I'M THE BOSS OF ME!

Stay Sexy, Smart & Strong at Any Age

by Joan Moran

To my family who loves and supports me unconditionally

To my sons Jonathan and Aaron

To my daughters-in-law: Carli and Alyse

*To my beautifully exuberant grandchildren:
Jordan, Luc, Jude, Greyson and Penelope*

*And a special and loving thank you to my developmental editor:
Emily Chase Smith*

Without Emily, I'm The Boss of Me! would never have happened.

CONTENTS

INTRODUCTION

Early in my 20 years of practicing yoga, I learned that a headstand was the king of all postures. Doing a headstand was better than the fountain of youth and more powerful than Botox.

I used to stand on my head all the time as a kid. I even stood on my head to get pregnant with my first child. After sexual intimacy with my husband, I leapt out of bed and kicked up my legs to the wall so one of his millions of sperm would attach to one of my eggs. That was two years of hard labor. Repeat for the second child.

I hoped my party trick headstand would make my mother forget I wasn't a piano prodigy and never was going to be considered for part of the San Francisco Ballet dance corps. Cheerleading and volleyball suited me better. I thank my lucky stars my mom told me to follow my heart and say *Yes* to what mattered most to me.

I continued doing headstands throughout my 20 years as a gym rat. After the aerobics craze, I stumbled into a yoga class at a boutique gym in Venice. I was familiar with yoga having practiced it and Transcendental Meditation in the late 1960s when the Hippie movement began to hold sway over popular culture. It came back into my life at just the right time.

The natural holistic practice of yoga allowed me to connect my busy mind with my busy body. The practice was not just amazingly joyful, but my headstand finally found a home. When I took a yoga teacher training class at 60, mastering the handstand stumped me. I was afraid my wrists would snap. They didn't, but I was the very last one in my class to kick my legs up to the wall with the help of a kind and generous 20-year-old assistant. I said *yes* to the handstand, *yes* to the possibility of becoming a yoga teacher and once again took charge of my life!

I became a yoga teacher in a very crowded yoga landscape in the West Los Angeles area, teaching privately at studios while gathering a group of private clients and then walking into the UCLA Recreation Department and signing onto the yoga staff. It was that easy. I had a great résumé.

It was only later in further yoga training that I learned that standing on one's head symbolizes the full range of human potential. All is possible. There are no limits, no labels. The *Nos* are passé. I want to pursue the *Yeses* in life. I've followed the *yes* mantra for the last 60 years, saying *Yes* to headstands, and following my heart into the theater, teaching, acting, producing, screenwriting, novel writing, yoga and dancing Argentine Tango. I even wrote a memoir called *60, Sex & Tango, Confessions of a Beatnik Boomer.* It's about living life in all its possibilities.

A friend asked me recently, "What about the *Nos?* Shouldn't we learn to say *No* first?"

My belief is that if you can say *Yes*, you'll understand better when to say *No*. In fact, implicit in the *Yes* is the *No*. They're seemingly opposing forces of energy, but in a more profound sense, *Yes* and *No* blend together to become *one tantric moment in time*. I went on to proclaim some Zen philosophy to my friend, "Tantric means there are no borders, no constrictions, no obstacles, no extremes. All your needs will be met in that moment of *Yes* and you will see your destiny clearly."

IT'S ABOUT THE MESSAGE

When I began my speaking journey, I wanted an exciting opening, a *wow* statement. I took my cue from Gypsy Rose Lee, the famous mid-20th Century American burlesque stripper whose infamous quote still delights me, "You've got to have a gimmick."

Understanding that a headstand was not just a gimmick, but it also represents a physical and spiritual balance that was instrumental in my decision to begin all my speeches with a headstand – legs spread in the splits, and most importantly, sporting a pair of high heels. It's an eye-catcher, an *in your face gimmick*, an almost insane piece of bravado. It's the only time I pray, "Dear Lord, please let this work." I never know if it will until I'm up in the air – secure for 5 seconds flipping my high heels about like I'm doing the Hustle.

I do a headstand because I can. Every time I turn myself upside down, I find my balance. That's when I'm the bravest. That's when I'm the boss of me.

The mantra I've taken on during the last 5 years of my writing/blogging/speaking adventure is *be wise about your choices, be physically active, sustain your body-mind-spirit connection, and be willing to engage in* amazing possibilities. This mantra has given me strength and courage to take my journey, my *dharma*, my true path in life.

My mother was a huge proponent of the idea that possibilities could lead to opportunities. In fact, her journey of openness to new ideas provided a role model for me. She used to say, "*Never fear anything, Joanie. It's a waste of time. Besides, it's more fun to be surprised by life.*"

My mother turned every possibility into an opportunity, from being a secretary right out of high school in 1928, to fixing up duplexes in San Francisco, then on to making a more than middle class living in the Marin County housing market remodeling houses and building duplexes. After I moved to Las Vegas, she took a leap of faith and seized the opportunity to build single-family dwellings on a Las Vegas golf course. She was a huge success.

My parents' edifices still stand the test of time with their beauty and elegance. Throughout her journey, my mom stayed sexy, smart and strong. I used to call her the *Barbara Stanwyck of the Big Valley* (a 60s TV show) with her boots and riding crop. She died at 98 still a beautiful babe.

My mother was fearless and said *Yes* to challenges most of us find confusing or even scary. We are aware that possibilities may turn into opportunities, but we don't want to fail, be ridiculed or be criticized so we assess the possibilities "realistically." Failure isn't sexy in our culture. Winners are sexy.

Yet, we are all human. We are all afraid of the unknown. We are all hard wired not to see the positive in the negative. It's as if we almost expect a negative outcome and in order to protect that flawed mindset, we use self-sabotage as the default position. It's easier and quicker to say *No* because it requires no thought, no effort, and no risk.

None of us want to miss the exhilaration, energy and passion that are necessary ingredients for a life well lived. I can guarantee life won't be any fun if you fail to pursue your passions to the fullest, express your joy with abandon and develop a healthy curiosity. Let this book inspire you to say *Yes* and leapfrog over obstacles that get in the way of your happiness.

Everyone has a significant *Yes* that is remembered in perpetuity and I've had my fair share. In my memoir, *60, Sex & Tango, Confessions of A Beatnik Boomer,* I write about leaving Las Vegas after 18 years. While I had a significant career in the theatre and more than my fair share of familiarity with the mob in Las Vegas, my decision to move to Los Angeles was spurred by a failed marriage and a desire for a richer, more complete environment for my sons and for myself.

I said *Yes* to a life change without knowing what was to come. My mother's words echoed: "Never fear anything, Joanie."

THE DELUGE

But a more profound moment was yet to come – profound because I was 70, and people that age rarely make big changes. I've noticed retirees *book their lives* instead of *living their lives*.

"When's the next Caribbean cruise, Mabel?"

"I thought we just went on one, Jack. Next stop is Cabo San Lucas."

Is the Boomer Generation so afraid of making decisions that might change their life story, decisions that put them on another path and take them on the magical mystical tour of possibilities, that they only feel comfortable being spectators? What gives me hope are stories about people who enhance their lives by challenging the status quo. I wanted to be one of those people.

It was the summer of 2014, and I was in the middle of a 12-week teaching schedule at UCLA riding the elevator up to the Penthouse rooftop in the Math and Engineering Building with one of my yoga ladies.

Julie and I were standing side by side in relative silence. I was thinking about how many more times I was going to take that elevator up to the 8th Floor to teach my yoga class.

"So, are you moving to Austin?" Julie asked. "Everyone is talking about it. Have you decided? Are you making the big change?"

I looked at her incredulously because the thought of moving was never far from my mind those days.

"What's wrong? Cat got your tongue?" she laughed.

"It's like you're inside my head," I told her. "Witch that you are. The move's been probably two years in the making. You know my son lives in Austin with his wife and two of my grandchildren. I've got lots of friends there that want me to move.

"Great city," she replied. "Music, dance, energy..."

"Friendly people with y'all this and y'all that. It's great because everything I want to be around is in Austin, but I needed a sign. Do you remember the deluge in July? It was like Saul on the Road to Damascus – lighting struck me – well, really it was the torrential water blasting out of the main water vein in front of the UCLA John Wooden Center parking structure."

"I remember it well. I was warm and cozy in my office with my car parked in the other lot - not even concerned," she laughed gleefully.

"You're wicked! The water main exploded directly in front of my car as I was waiting to make a right turn into the garage. The water shot up from the descending ramp that leads into the parking garage and flooded Sunset Blvd. It was undeterred in its furry. If I had arrived just a few moments sooner, my brand new car would be buried in water with me struggling to find an exit. Of course, that didn't happen, but it was nonetheless prophetic being almost washed away by water. Cleansed and rebirthed."

"That's pretty heavy biblical stuff," Julie said with a twinkle in her eye.

"Yeah, because at that moment, I had a vision that my yoga journey at UCLA was over. My students and private clients would sustain their yoga paths without me and it was time to leave LA."

Shortly after that conversion and after thirty years of an amazing life in LA, at the age of 70, I became the boss of me once again and moved to Austin, Texas on January 26, 2015. I was making up the rules as I drove to Austin and it was an unbelievable rush. My life story just got better.

Because I said *Yes* and took a leap of faith, my daily rush now is that I am more in tune with myself. I'm not just another version of me; I'm living life through the lens of a deeper place inside of me. And from that deeper place comes an appreciation and a gratitude for time that is not defined, for change that is meaningful, and for self-reflection that brings knowledge, understanding and wisdom. Everyone can reach a deeper place inside themselves and find greater meaning. The possibilities are endless.

Who calls the shots now in your life? Who's the boss of you? Ambition, success and the super ego will not determine the quality of your life the way they did when you were young and momentum meant everything. Then it was an anathema to stop, sit, watch, contemplate and self-reflect. Your thoughts were toward changing the world and not toward better understanding yourself.

As you age you create another version of your personal dynamic. It's different for everyone, but you know it when you discover a more profound sense of self and purpose. It's alchemy. It's magic. The dice land on the crap table of life, but in a different combination.

STOP THE WORLD, I WANT TO GET OFF

Yet there's a persistent problem in our culture now. The majority of people fail to look inside themselves for answers to their deepest issues. It's no fun to be mindful about your struggles when distractions are everywhere. People, places and things hold you back, get in the way of your happiness and keep you stuck in quicksand. Your thinking gets small and the size of your thinking determines the size of your results.

During my years of studying yoga, I discovered a large body of spiritual thought and philosophy from the Sutras, the Vedas, Buddhist wisdom (particularly, *The Tibetan Book of Living and Dying*), and my yoga gurus, to Eckhart Tolle, Wayne Dwyer, Maya Angelou and websites that speak to *walking the path of spiritual awakening, the importance of empowering women, finding balance in all aspects of life* and *learning how to make great decisions.*

All great thinkers, all empowering gurus and all thought leaders support the power of now – staying 100% mindfully in the present moment. The present will tell you everything you need to know about where you want to go next.

It's time to slip into something more comfortable, like consciousness.

I'm a compulsive blogger. After writing more than 200 blogs, I stopped counting. I worry about why I write so many blogs. Is something wrong with me? My former Jungian therapist would undoubtedly say, "It's perfectly normal for you, Joan. Keep writing. It gives you clarity. And keep dreaming because those dreams will tell you why you write." I loved that man!!

I've never had much clarity. Whenever I think I have it, masses of self-doubt creep into my psyche. I never come out and directly *say* what I want, need or desire because I write it better. It's paradoxical – self-doubt is the reason I write and the way I stay strong in mind, body and spirit.

Today's zeitgeist proposes that bloggers publish their blogs in book form. What a coincidence! I believe I have gathered sufficient philosophic content and real life experiences to create a book of my blogs – a book that might stimulate, enlighten and even instruct readers to live life to the fullest and be their own boss.

HERE'S THE CHALLENGE!

All of us are truly blessed. We humans have been given the power to develop ideas and exercise free will. This ability helps us understand our relationship to the world at large. It allows us to reject the negative, the angry or the violent. Our free will allows us to discriminate and open our heart. It keeps us free of ego domination. It lets us defy labels and judgments that get in the way of clear thinking.

We continually face challenges in life, and that's a good thing because challenges help us grow, transform and stay sexy, smart and strong.

To face challenges, grow, and to take charge of your life, consider a few simple but effective tools to guide you along the path of self-reflection. I call these tools *Mind Fuel Tools for Life Renewal.*

These tools provide context for living. They'll start you thinking more pro-actively about your life, reduce stress and resistance, open your mind up to new ideas, get rid of rigid responses, self-important opinions, and put the ego mind in its proper place. Imagine how it will feel to embrace a universe that looks differently, thinks differently, and feels differently.

The Mind Fuel tools will also provide context for you as you read this book. They are the window and the reference frame through which you will *be the boss of you*, learn to take charge of your life and stay sexy, smart and strong at any age.

5 MIND FUEL TOOLS FOR LIFE RENEWAL

1   *Have an attitude of gratitude:* We are on this earth and our life is our gift. Surely you can say thank you for your life, your breath. Every religion talks about the importance of gratitude in life, but sometimes we don't hear the message clearly. Meister Eckhart, a 13th Century mystic, wrote: "If the only prayer we said throughout our lives was thank you, that would suffice."

   Gratitude is an awareness that everything that makes your life creative and loving will inspire and empower you to give more of yourself. Gratitude says, "I am sufficient to the needs of my own life." Gratitude builds your dreams and establishes your foundation in work and in life.

2   *Be Vulnerable:* Vulnerability gives emotional connection and expands the imagination. In a profound way, the path to self-

reflection is embracing vulnerability. *It is at the moment you become emotionally openly honest* that creativity takes hold. Vulnerability allows your imagination to soar and you are open to new and exciting ideas. Vulnerability allows you to act with consciousness, empathy, sympathy, and generosity of spirit.

3 *Learn to Adapt:* Making changes to your life and adapting to them is an art and a science. To make the changes necessary to your well being you need to be living in the present, otherwise you'll miss the opportunity to seize the change.

The way to adapt is to understand that the only opinion worth anything is your own because it comes from the truth inside of you. How do we find our truth? Abu Said, a famous 14th century Sufi poet in the Persian Empire, answers, "Take one step away from yourself-and lo behold! – the path."

Our Sufi poet is advising us to get out of the way of ourselves so we can see our lives more clearly. I call this the 10% solution. In order to get perspective, detach 10% from the situation and you will see the necessary change.

4 *Find Passion:* My mother, a woman defined by her passions, described passion as an outpouring of positive energy for the interests and ideas that made a difference in her life.

Another way of finding passion comes from the words of Margaret Mead: "Don't ask yourself what the world needs. Ask yourself what makes you come alive and then go and do that because what the world needs are people who have come alive."

5 *Practice Forgiveness:* If we're honest, we acknowledge that we have all harbored resentments, collected injustices, and have be-

come angry over unimportant insults. I meditate. I burn candles. I drink green tea. And I still want to smack someone who offends me.

It is challenging and completely exasperating to forgive someone – it might even be harder to forgive yourself. Forgiving is about letting go, surrendering, and moving forward. Forgiving not only clears the mind of negativity, but it is also crucial in resolving issues, communicating more effectively, providing empathy, and living a happier life. Without forgiveness there would be no history, no hope, and our species would have annihilated itself in endless retributions.

SO LET'S GO FOR IT!

Writing this book of blogs has taught me that the real definition of having it all is when what you *want* and what you *have* match up. It's like an eclipse of the sun, but this magical time lasts longer then 7 minutes and 31 seconds.

Having it all involves the freedom to seize the moment, like eating pizza in bed, dancing around in your underwear to the Bee Gees' *Staying Alive* or undressing to Donna Summers singing *Last Dance*. On one occasion, having it all meant I stopped going to Buenos Aires to dance tango for the 14th time and took off for Costa Rica to walk the rain forests. It was liberating. I had it all again when I hopped on a plane to Bali with two of my friends and with no idea what was going to happen. It's different for everyone, but you know it when you have it.

I hope you find something in a blog or two that gives you understanding coupled with masses of wisdom. I encourage you to read the blogs a few at a time and not inhale all of them at once. This method worked well with Eckhart Tolle's widely read book, *The*

Power of Now. Reading only 2 or 3 sections a night before I went to bed made it easier to digest, and I could focus on the message by reading each section several times over. Take your time and see where your thoughts take you.

Some of these blogs will cover topics that interest you, other blogs may amuse or inspire change that is long overdue. Perhaps one of them will give you the courage to make a great decision about your life. The list is long, but I hope the journey is fun.

PART 1
Stay Sexy

You've heard it before, *You get better as you age.* Is that phrase a fabrication of modern consumerism and/or a constant and true axiom of life? Is that mantra intended to push us to try to look ten years younger with a face-lift, a pill or a personal trainer?

Heck, no! There are no such things as quick fixes. If you are mindful, curious and happy, you do get better with age. You become more and more sexy, smart, strong, vibrant, and energetic. There is no expiration date on who you are.

The mindset that you slow down as you get into your 60s or even 70s is just phooey. At 72 I'm more energetic and *out there* than ever before. I have no complaints and few regrets, if any. I can only think of maybe 5 men I shouldn't have had sex with over the years and I don't hold it against them – the sex just wasn't special enough.

Being sexy doesn't stop when you hit a particular age. I can attest to that fact. Older women are sexy and interesting in a wise way. We listen, have great empathy, love deeply, and have a certain *je ne sais quoi* attitude about living fully and well. Throw in a little lust, and older attractive women are a precious commodity. The French understand that concept. Americans don't.

There's not much to celebrate in literature about the allure of older women. In our so-called American milieu nobody cares much. By Hollywood's cultural standards we're not attractive enough, sexy enough or even smart enough. I've always wanted to write books for women who have a strong and commanding presence in our times, but thank Venus, Eric Jong beat me to it.

In *Fear of Dying,* Jong wrote a book about an older woman who is sexual, attractive and wants to reach out for life. Hey!! That's me! What a concept!! We do exist. Ms. Jong said, "That's not celebrated, sadly, and I would hope that a lot of older women who read this book realize that sex doesn't disappear, it just changes forms."

Fear of Dying lands in the middle of a long-festering debate about the social and cultural obstacles older women face. For all anyone cares, an aging woman's desirability could dissipate in a single day. Sex therapists and gurus have published dozens of manuals and self-help books with titles like *Sex for Seniors* and *Sex Over 50.* There is also the gag book, *Sex After 60,* which is entirely blank inside. I'm spilling over with laughter.

But the subject of the glorious offerings older women contribute to the world hasn't been widely explored in popular fiction. "Women were not allowed to have passion at 60," Ms. Jong writes in *Fear of Dying.* "We were supposed to become grandmothers and retreat into serene sexlessness."

"There is this giant void in the culture about women in that age group as heroines, as romantic beings, as sexual beings and as creative beings, and there's not that void for men," said Naomi Wolf, author of *The Beauty Myth.* "Women don't stop being all those things as their lives continue into those decades."

Women are amazing creations! We have been mythologized, idealized, idolized, lionized, patronized, held up as paragons of virtue and painted as fallen angels. Women are nurturers by nature with nuanced sensibilities that reflect our unique intelligence. If we're on our game, fully conscious and particularly mindful, the life we live on the outside reflects our inside life – our dreams and passions. We know that growth and transformation are necessary for reaching our human potential and that includes claiming the highest level of our well being. Harmonious relationships are the gateway for manifesting our desires. Aren't we fabulous! Aren't we sexy, smart and strong!

LET'S DO THE TWIST
Come on baby, let's do the twist
Come on baby, let's do the twist
Take me by my little hand and go like this
Eh ah twist baby, baby twist
Oh yeah just like this
Come on little miss and do the twist
- From *Let's Do The Twist* sung by Chubby Checker

A BEATNIK BOOMER: LIVING HAPPY, WILD & FREE

My life has been a series of happy journeys. I've always felt I had a good handle on the way things were going and that most of my choices were creative. I was fortunate to have walked down many interesting and challenging roads – an actress, entrepreneur, writer, theater professor, yoga instructor and tango dancer. The best road I've taken is being a mother to two incredible sons and a grandmother to five awesome grandchildren. What's not to like about my life?

But sometime in my early 60s I realized I might not have the necessary tools or skill set to handle living large in my 60s. My disturbing wake-up call at age 63 is not unique to baby boomers. Back in the 1960s, we didn't trust anyone over 30 and completely ignored anyone over 40. I deduced that I wasn't alone in thinking that turning 60 can be an extremely difficult concept to grasp for boomers who thought of themselves as eternally youthful, hip and cool.

I'm not a boomer by technical definition. I was born in 1943, so I missed the start by a few years, but my heart and soul was always aligned with the Beatnik Generation. The beatniks and existentialists infused my philosophy of life. In a strange way, I'm still that 19-year-old girl in Berkeley believing the world holds infinite promise and hope. Then, the world as we knew it changed in '68

5

and with it the destination of our generation changed drastically and forever. It was a watershed year.

The hippie generation arrived, and with hipster flair, I found myself spanning two incredibly seminal literary and social movements. I went from being a beatnik, adoring Jack Kerouac, to being a hippie and worshiping the Beatles. In fact, I was working at the Sahara Hotel in Las Vegas in 1964 when the Beatles landed in a helicopter on the rooftop. At the time, I was faking my way into a marriage and faking my way into a job as a secretary – I had no skills for either.

Then life happened and time gave me the opportunity to pursue my dreams in theater and live a complete and exciting life. I was determined to live my Beatnik life and carry forward what I set out to do. Along the way, I taught high school and college, wrote a couple of textbooks on acting and had 2 sons. After 18 years I left Las Vegas, a marriage that wasn't working and a dream that wasn't fulfilled. The boys and I grew up together and managed to create some semblance of normality.

The moment I became a grandmother for the first time, I was jolted out of my complacency. I encountered emotions and fears that were alien to me. It had been decades since I raised children. I didn't even like babies, but these new beings were part of my growing family. I thought I wasn't going to be good enough or able enough to take on the role of grandmother. At the same time, I was dealing with the impending passing of my mother and the death of my significant other. I feared the loss of control. Was I strong enough to be the boss of me?

I began to wrestle with the idea of embracing aging gracefully and rejecting becoming old and boring. I deeply wanted to continue to possess the youthful 19-year-old spirit that fought bravely for individual identity and independence.

As writers do, I began to put down my thoughts. When I started my memoir, I never envisioned it would be published, but my self-deprecating humor and lots of red wine carried me through and I began to think that someone might want to read it – someone with a sense of humor and an understanding of irony.

I was living my life and writing about it at the same time. Trying to parent my adult children wasn't working. Another son got married, more grandchildren appeared, and I started Internet dating. Gasp! Then, of all the absurd decisions, I decided to become a yoga teacher to reach nirvana as I continued to make multiple trips to Buenos Aires to dance tango like an addicted drug user.

I learned a lot about myself writing my memoir and I learned even more from my yoga gurus and yoga practice. I began to understand that struggle is overrated and that personal and spiritual growth is an ongoing process that would always bring me joy. I realized that as we grow older, we have to work diligently at pursuing our individuality and sense of self. I learned that mindfulness is a way to stay fully present, gain self-knowledge and improve communication.

It's important that boomers reject clichés about getting older and continue to see life as full of possibilities and opportunities. If boomers can maintain an energetic and positive attitude about living large, chronological age is superfluous. Health will improve, the mind will stay strong and you will look and be as sexy as ever.

I've always been a happy and positive person, yet aging requires a new mindset that I didn't always practice in my 60s. As I approached my 70s, I had to learn how to become an even happier, more positive and grateful person. I count my blessings every day and feel fortunate that my personal happiness is augmented by an exuberant family, and a passion for yoga, meditation and Argentine tango. All that combined with the ability to laugh at myself means I never take myself too seriously and keeps me living happy, wild and free.

Pun Intended – It's Still Sexy

This next piece of writing isn't a blog, but it is a stand-up comedy routine I performed several years ago at the Westside Comedy Club in Santa Monica. There is nothing sexier than a senior citizen talking about sex. I kid. Well, maybe I don't kid because sex at any age is a wonderful and fascinating experience.

The house was packed and the comedy was met with hilarity. Everyone should do at least one stand-up routine in life. It's truly liberating.

Ever notice when senior sex is mentioned in conversation it's a buzz kill?

My ex-boyfriend, a 72-year-old rocker dude and reserve sheriff told me a story about riding in a patrol car. The macho sheriffs were talking about sex. My ex-boyfriend stopped them cold, "I guess you guys didn't get laid last night. I did and it was the best sex I ever had." We broke up 2 weeks later.

It wasn't because sex wasn't great. A daily Cialis and a senior guy will make good every time. Unfortunately, he had temper tantrums like an adolescent.

Are you thinking that senior sex is gross? Don't knock it if you haven't tried it. Sex at any age with any man can be gross; seniors don't have the market cornered. But senior sex can sometimes involve a lot more intimacy, a lot more than, well, just plan cold, hard sex. Speaking of cold, hard senior sex...it exists.

Back when I was 62 and very single, I had a senior yoga client who was a crack addict. Of course yoga and crack go together. Why not?

My client was also a sex addict and I was fascinated because I was curious as to how she got so much sex. She fed her addiction with online adult sites (that's code for more than *friendly* dating services). She had sex slaves come over to give her pleasure and play with her large collection of mechanical dildos, which were scarier than shit. She had senior sex down pat. Of course, her tastes were different than mine. Intimacy was what I was after.

My client thought I needed to get laid. She wondered if I even had a libido.

"I've got very good libido," I said. "Don't worry about me."

Once convinced, she signed me up for online dating. First up: JDate, the dating site for finding a good Jewish husband. She lied about my age. The thought of dating made me nauseous, but lying about my age seemed like a good idea at the time. Turns out I love Jewish men in the abstract, but not in real time. They're too much work.

My first Jewish date made an appearance in front of Starbucks. Ben was slightly balding and wore shorts & dock shoes. The look was deadly. I almost made an about face.

"Are you a Jewess?" he asked with a knowing smile. I nodded with apprehension. I guess I passed the test.

I practically had to beg him for something to eat at Starbucks. "What'dya want?" he asked.

"Carrot cake," I told him. Carrot cake's considered foreplay for a Jew. Ten minutes later, he got tired of seeing me eat and threw it in the garbage. I actually got sexually aroused. We were in bed a half hour later.

We stayed in bed for 3 days and then he asked me to marry him. I told him we should wait at least a week or my sons would disown me, my brother would commit me to an asylum – but my mother would love me again. She never got over my divorce from my Jewish husband who had money.

Marriage never happened. We were off and on for 4 years. During our timeouts, I dated on Match.com, Yahoo & eHarmony. Enough Jews. I was into gentile sociopaths.

A self-obsessed/self-absorbed stockbroker asked me if I lied about my age and I guiltily said yes. He launched into a rant about women who lie. I was trying to eat a dry salad at the worst deli in LA (yes, there are bad delis in LA) while he ate nothing because he didn't eat after 5 pm. It went against the rules of his workout diet. I felt like a midget in a straight jacket. It was excruciating.

A screenwriter/teacher who cancelled our New Year's Eve date ended up in Thailand getting a tsunami up his ass. He would have been better off having sex with me rather than a high colonic in Asia.

There were other types of dysfunction too – guys who really wanted to date their daughters instead of grown women.

One guy asked me if I would show him the results of my AIDS test. Who asks that on a first date?

Joey Suitcase, the Sicilian, hacked my email for a year. I think all that testosterone he injected turned him into a werewolf. His balls had shrinkage.

I found out how sex works if you have prostate cancer: shoot some fun liquid into your penis and it lasts *forever* (so annoying after about 3 hours). If you don't take your Viagra a couple of hours before you want to get laid, the woman may not wait around until you get hard. Adios, amigo. I hit the trail.

In the intervening years, I've been somewhat more selective about having senior sex. Am I mellowing? Maybe. Have I lost my sex drive? Not quite. I will still make love to a special man even though that man may not hold an erection as long as I would want. I try not to fixate on the good old days when sex marathons were as common as discos. But senior men find that cuddling, holding hands, laughing, spooning and kissy facing can be ever so gratifying. If there is a sexual thrill, it's in the nuanced details.

A while back I met a man in Florida, an adorable 70-year-old, good body, a passionate dancer and very sexy. The first time we made love it wasn't so good, but he was super attentive to my needs. The second time was spot on and he said to me with a twinkle in his eye, "Some days are better than others." That's senior sex in a nutshell.

"Someday he'll come along,
the man I love
And he'll be big and strong,
the man I love
And when he comes my way,
I'll do my best to make him stay.
- From *The Man I Love* by George Gershwin

LOVE AFTER 60

As I come to the end of the decade of my 60s, I have been musing about the state of love, men and lack thereof in my life. In my early 60s, I wrote a memoir entitled, *60, Sex & Tango, Confessions of a Beatnik Boomer*, in which I wrote riffs on my life as a single woman, mother of adult sons, a grandmother, a part-time lover and internet dater. I was also looking for a profound and loving relationship.

As I struck out in the love department, I asked myself, "Was I looking for love in all the wrong places? Did the men I choose for a time, 4 in all, suit my personality and what kind of man did I desire during my aging Baby Boomer journey?" Obviously, these 4 men did not fill the bill. Some lasted a year or more. Others didn't even make it that long.

Yet, it did occur to me that love after 60 requires women to alter attitudes, perceptions and most importantly, *clarify their intentions*. The old-fashioned concept of love where the white knight saves the damsel in distress doesn't work anymore.

Don't just fill your dance card: fill your needs.

Thinking about love after 60 requires continuous self-reflection, which leads to self-knowledge and assured confidence. Self-reflection also helps get rid of self-doubt, which leads to: *I'm the boss of me!*

My therapist told me love is a mystery. There is no rhyme or reason to its hold on our emotions. One loves passionately, or not at all. But as a single woman dating in my 60s, I deduced a few things about single men (divorced, widowed or never married) and their changing social conventions.

A single man needs to be free of encumbrances (family, children, past loves) in order to individuate and love completely.

A single man needs to be sufficiently connected to his own vulnerability in order to fall in love with a woman.

A single man needs to contribute in equal ways to growing a relationship in which the needs of the couple are met.

A single man needs to be generous with his time and means and not feel deprived financially, emotionally or psychologically.

By the time I hit the decade of my 60s, I was convinced both genders signed off on a new economic parity. Voila! The dating game changed. The disparity of money and unrealized economic expectations for both men and women blurred the traditional dating conventions of the 1950s, 1960s and even into the 1970s. By the end of the 1980s, the ritual of a man taking a woman out on a date and paying was beginning to look like a quaint idea.

The typical dating situation looks a little like a cat and mouse game. If you are dating retired or close to retirement, it's common that both genders feel each other out on financial issues faster than any other topic. If a single man in his 60s senses you have a retirement fund or some significant money in the bank, he might suggest splitting the evening's entertainment. He doesn't know you, he doesn't love you, and he won't get sex from you on the first date anyway. Even if he does get sex from you, he might expect you to pay for dinner while he picks up the tab for the room.

I had this situation happen to me in the reverse. I planned on treating my companion and I to Cirque du Soleil during our few days in Las Vegas. He would pick up the other expenses. I booked the room using my credit card and at checkout, my date pulled a fast one and let my card stand for a night's charges. I made him reimburse me. It turned out I didn't have enough money for his tastes and he gratefully dumped me. I was a happy camper.

When it comes to lifestyles and financial means, there can be conflict. A man's relationship to money is complicated and it can interfere with a loving relationship. A woman's relationship to her needs and desires can interfere with a loving commitment. The dating experience gets complicated when you can't let go of unrealized expectations and personal perception.

Love after 60 requires nurturing and that lends itself to a greater understanding of needs, expectations and aspirations. It is also valuable for both genders to assess the idiosyncrasies, character flaws, damaged psyches, resentments, emotional baggage and cultural dispositions that impact the relationship. Trust, honest communication and clear intentions help keep a relationship on track. Love after 60 can flourish, but there is no doubt that it requires a big leap of faith.

WHAT'S YOUR STORY, MORNING GLORY?

When I'm not in a relationship I miss the energy of love. I miss the touching. I miss whispering in a man's ear some girlie secret feeling. There are so many things I miss about being in love I cannot even count the ways.

Yet, I know that love is complicated. Love's core is defined by a central question: How do you have a committed relationship over time while maintaining your own personal happiness and integrity? If you understand that being in love means sharing and giving, being open and vulnerable, honest and communicative, love is perfectly doable. Of course, this is a huge personal and collective challenge and commitment.

A few months ago, a friend of mine came to Los Angeles to visit family. He spends three months in LA then returns to the city where he resides. We found each other on the tango floor, we both have a passion for Argentine tango, and we liked each other more than a lot. There was an obvious attraction. While we were getting to know each other, we talked about what it means to have a committed relationship at our age.

While we spoke, I had a comforting feeling that our maturity made us connect more directly in the present moment. At times it felt like shorthand. Both of us lived 60 plus decades, collected many unique experiences, made mistakes, had successes and were embraced by our children and grandchildren. We had moved through many similar changes and it seemed as if we could make our own rules about what a partnership would look like in the future.

In my vision of coupling, when love is seasoned, both partners keep up with the changes in each other's lives.

Lillian Hellman wrote: *People change and forget to tell each other.*

For those who come to love later in life, it takes time to have sufficient past information to feel comfortable in the love zone. We don't know what he/she was like 20 or 30 years ago and we have to incorporate present and past in order to anchor and secure a truly intimate relationship.

Adults who embrace a loving relationship find it requires positive energy, fortitude, and patience. It requires an understanding of how to be intimate and how to keep the relationship playful. Couples bond more closely when they do new and exciting things together. Activities such as taking a painting class, opening up a bed and breakfast, signing up for the Peace Corp, exercising, taking regular yoga classes and meditating invigorate love and spread joy and gratitude.

The man I met talked the talk, unfortunately, he didn't walk the walk. Did I mention commitment?

....

ALL YOU NEED IS LOVE
There's nothing you can do that can't be done.
Nothing you can sing that can't be sung.
Nothing you can say but you can learn how to play the game.
It's easy.
- From *All You Need Is Love* by the Beatles

....

LOVE YOURSELF FIRST — GETTING THE MOST FROM LIFE AFTER 60

Lucille Ball said it: *"Love yourself first and everything else falls into line."* Loving yourself first contributes to a positive and joyful attitude in life. It's too easy to default to the negative mindset that is nurtured by our hectic environment and culture. We've got so much going on that finding ways to keep our life balanced and healthy takes Herculean effort.

You know what it's like to feel off balance from time to time. When things don't go well, we have a queasy feeling in our stomachs. Thornton Wilder, one of the great playwrights of the 20th century, had a line in his wonderful play, *The Skin of Our Teeth*, which I still recite today although I played the lunatic maid, Sabina decades ago. "The world's at sixes and sevens!" I have absolutely no idea what that means, but it's crazy enough to lend credence to my sometimes off-kilter condition.

How do we re-connect and re-discover our authentic self? If you're anything like me, I can't seem to see the forest through the trees when it comes to my emotional connections. I may look cool and collected, but I'm a mess inside. My focus is off, a lump is tickling my throat and my dreams are creepy. I have anxiety over being anxious. What in the world is going to happen next?

The fears we produce over and over again keep us stuck in the quicksand of our own making. Do we have the patience to wait until our mud settles? Can we remain unmoved until the right action comes along?

The answer is yes if we love ourselves first, are true to our values and know that we are simply part of the spectrum of a life that we are making – the great, big, wonderful life we are living in in the present. I think that's sexy.

It takes decades of processing our lives to regain our strength, to find balance and be the best that we can be. It takes a considerable thought, more than a little patience and some old-fashioned tenacity, resourcefulness and resilience to keep loving ourselves.

Here are a few ways to practice self-love:

Follow your heart
The one brilliant piece of advice my Jungian therapist gave me in my year of therapy was: follow your heart.

Be true to yourself
If you know who you are and acknowledge the truth of your journey, your dharma, there will be no struggle.

Create your own status in society
Dance as if no one is watching.

Apply no blame to others
We are responsible only to ourselves; we make the choices.

Prioritize what's important
Begin every day by doing the most important thing – something that promotes positive energy, lights your fire or adds to your knowledge.

Have confidence in your abilities
We know we have everything inside us to be the best that we can be.

Cultivate curiosity
It's how we learn and grow.

Be surprised
You'll be delighted.

Find compassion and forgiveness in all things
The positive energy will be a prevailing force to ensure balance.

Have an attitude of gratitude
Gratitude will inspire your life and create abundance and positive energy for living.

It only takes one – you – to be happy and fulfilled.

I recently attended a tango festival over Labor Day Weekend in my hometown of Austin, Texas. It was cool, funky, and full of colors and styles. This was the most perfect festival I'd attended in 20 years and I felt marvelous as I danced for three days.

A friend of mine for more than a decade asked me to dance – a beautiful and elegant dancer who is also a teacher and a DJ. I was honored and full of anticipation and joy. After the first tango, my friend looked at me intensely.

"What's wrong?" he asked.

"Nothing," I replied. "I'm simply happy."

"That's it?" he responded. "Happy?"

I smiled with a twinkle in my eyes. "Perfectly happy."

At that moment, I felt perfect the way I was – and perfectly happy.

"That's kind of sexy," he added with a smile.

What is the amazing ingredient that makes me perfect? It's not just about dancing tango, it can also be grocery shopping in the middle of an Austin afternoon when my skin burns from the heat, or when I'm out of breath from pushing my bike up a hill covered in gravel rocks, or even when I completely forget that I'm not wearing eye makeup, which years ago would have sent me into a panic.

Why do I feel perfect as I grow older, grayer with fingers no longer strong enough to twist off bottle caps without effort?

What if everything about me was perfect from the beginning and I didn't know it? What if all those years of struggle to be gloriously happy were simply a movie that played in my head and had no relevance to my real life?

The Buddhists say we are born with all the happiness we will ever need or want. Ironically, it's human nature that stops that mantra from manifesting.

Yet, if you are perfect and there is no struggle, how do you grow and transform? Aren't you supposed to take yourself on as a project? Isn't your life your life's work?

And what about everything else, the people, places and things that are part of the spectrum called *your life*? Where do they fit in? If you are not aware and conscious of all that life holds, how can you expect perfection and joy?

As I mused about how I felt the last night of the tango festival, I wondered how I had arrived at such a delicious state of *I'm perfect*. I believe it was years in the making. It was my confidence in taking risks, making glorious mistakes and plenty of leaps of faith. It was heaps of acceptance and gratitude for the way I turned out in life; I'm a happy woman because I am who I am and no one else was responsible for that except me.

The truth of your perfection comes in knowing the truth about yourself, finding your energy and light and reflecting your true sense of self with love and inspiration.

My life is my work and I am the one who discovered all the jewels in the being called Joan. Joan made me laugh, made me ponder with wonderment and made me leave a footprint on this planet.

AMAZING FACTS YOU CAN LEARN FROM YOURSELF IF YOU JUST SHOW UP

Today is everyday and everyday is an opportunity to learn something fabulous about who you are.

Think of your life as a giant goodie basket. You can use everything in the goodie basket to your advantage, such as engaging life's challenges head on, meeting important needs, making significant connections or finding personal and professional success. Life is a day-by-day opportunity if you simply show up.

The cool thing about your life is that you don't have to justify it to anyone else. Will people support your life's decisions all the time? No, they won't. Will people walk in your shoes? No, they won't. Will people align themselves with your philosophical needs, desires and values? No, they won't. Your life is yours alone.

So take a pass on those who criticize, judge or label your authentic self. Your mantra is and always will be: "I respectfully do not care." Or, as Rhett Butler said in *Gone With The Wind*, "Frankly, my dear, I don't give a damn!"

Yet, it's human nature to seek information outside your amazing self. You've heard countless presentations on how to reinvent your life and how to increase your happiness quotient. You've read 20 books on dialing down stress and managing emotions. You've asked therapists to help you self-actualize and you've paid life coaches to help you craft life decisions and build momentum to meet your goals. You've consulted gurus and clairvoyants to give you the magic answer to the truths of your life.

George Bernard Shaw wrote: *Life isn't about finding yourself. Life is about creating yourself.*

The moment of creation begins when you discover the one thing you want most in life and then master it. Once you discover that one thing, the rest of your life is about self-mastery – living the same wholehearted and happy life every day as your conscious awareness meets the "nitty-gritty."

Here are 5 amazing things you can learn about yourself by living a conscious and wholehearted life:

1   *Your conscious mind leads you to right intention.*
    Everyone has difficulty making the right decisions. Sometimes even the goals you set are not compatible with what you want to accomplish in life. That happens when the right intention isn't clear. You may be tied to old mental categories and habits that get in the way of what you really want, need, and desire. Live

consciously and press the reset button. The right intention will be at your fingertips.

2   *Your conscious mind helps you strategize about your life.*
Your conscious mind helps you negotiate complex social relationships and environments. Consciousness measures your social awareness and evolves social beliefs and attitudes. Only you can be a disciple of the things that interest you and be aware of the meaning and significance in life. At first, it may seem daunting, but time is always on your side.

3   *Your conscious mind helps manage fear.*
You are the only person who can acknowledge your fears and release them from your unconscious mind. When that happens, your conscious mind can manage your fears; that's when you recognize the possibility of personal growth. Turning the negative energy of fear into positive energy of abundance changes your mindset about the unknown.

4   *Your conscious mind connects the 18 inches between your head and heart.*
The flow of mind to heart is an amazing phenomenon. It's an awesome concept that you "think with the mind of your heart." The heart is a powerful energy center that represents a generosity of spirit, forgiveness, love and passion. Your heart center is the spirit and truth allowing you to learn from your emotions, even the negative ones. Emotions enable you to telescope the truth of who you are, recognize the feelings about how you live, learn and relate to others.

5   *Your conscious mind makes great decisions.*
Your conscious mind is the most important tool available to you. As a result, you can give your full attention to making deci-

sions that are right for you. Segmented thinking results in confusing decisions. Great decisions come from a quiet mind, one that is not distracted by mindless messages and its environment.

You are the creator of your actions and thoughts. You have everything inside of you necessary to live with fulfillment and joy. Learn from yourself and trust in your capacity to build an awesome life.

....

WASTE NOT, WANT NOT, YOU SEXY THING
I got chills - they're multiplyin'
And I'm losin' control
Cause the power you're supplyin'
It's electrifyin'.
- From Grease - You're the One That I Want

....

YOU'RE THE ONE THAT I WANT

For those of you who don't know (but who doesn't know?), *You're the One That I Want* is a song from the movie, *Grease*. Danny Zuko loves Sandy, she's the one he wants. Ah, young love and all that jazz.

How many times a day do we say: *That's what I want. That's what I need. I've always wanted this!"*

Mindless mental riffing on self-gratification, either emotional or material, leads to more mindless repetition and mindless repetition is a real brain killer. Your brain gets stuck in a loop. In the meantime, what's going on with the other 99% of your brain?

Come on, humans, let's do the math on the possibilities of using the full capacity and potential of our brains. We could rock the world instead of stagnating. We could even get close to maximizing our human potential.

I was babysitting two of my grandsons in Las Vegas in the month of June. It was record-breaking heat, and I had been in the city twice that month so I was over it. I was hanging in the third rung of hell.

I'm always mesmerized by my 3½-year-old grandson repeating: "I want. I want. I want." I want what I want what I want. Dang. I love the kid - he's tough, resilient, stubborn, all boy, the typical 3-year-old narcissist. Everything in life reflects back to Jude as in "Hey, Jude!"

Ever notice that our *wants* don't move our lives forward? As in: I want my old boyfriend back in another incarnation, but it's over and there is no more joy in it. I want the love of my life back to complete our relationship, but he has left the earth and we already fulfilled our destiny together. I want my mother to be here for me and see her beauty shine at 98, but she was ready to leave her life. I want Sundays to be shared with friends, but Sundays alone are often the best moments of my week.

You want so many things in life that you could spend what time you have left on earth in the wanting zone. *What you really want is not to want.* It's difficult to see when our consumer culture constantly sucks us into material and emotional wanting.

One thing about aging I've discovered is that you want less. People over 65 are considered invisible to marketers because we don't buy into idealized love or purchase unnecessary material goods unless we are super-motivated to return to the past or still follow cultural trends.

I just cleaned out my apartment after 15 years and I wanted less and less of what was in it because my focus and needs have changed. I got rid of more and am living lighter than before. Recycling the good stuff is mindful thinking.

Sometimes I play a game with myself as I walk through a mall looking for nothing in particular. I see something I really adore and then examine it and ask if I really want it and why I need it. Unless it's a one-of-a-kind thing that will change my life, make me stretch my mind or increase my joy quotient, the wanting goes away.

Material things never last; lastingness and legacy come from the heart, from a loving family, from finding passion and experiencing joy.

We know this in theory but, still, it's the mindlessness of human brain activity that often prevails. If you want less, you need less and you'll live with less. That's the path to take charge of your life and stay sexy, smart and strong at any age.

LOVE THE ONE YOU'RE WITH: YOU'RE WORTH IT

The one thing I hear daily from friends, yoga students and family is, "I wish I had more time for me." This seems to be a ubiquitous observation that is repeated many times over on daytime talk shows, in health and wellness articles, women's magazines and from almost everyone who is concerned about work/life balance.

Is your mind so very busy, so full of *stuff*, so anxious to do the next activity that clearing the mind seems antithetical to creating your life in a meaningful way? Is everything in life equally important, every value the same?

Change your mindset and give yourself the gift of time:

Practice making intentions
Intentions give you permission to take care of your personal needs and desires on a daily basis. Almost everything you do or say takes place below the level of awareness so it's crucial that you stay fully present when making clear intentions. The present will tell you everything you need to know about what your next step will be.

In my yoga teacher training class, my master teacher made a suggestion to assist in the practice of mindful awareness and making intentions. Set your phone to ring every hour or so and at that time either continue your present intention or change it as desired. That's a great way to always practice awareness.

Get rid of mindless activities
I am hearing from more of my friends lately that they have cancelled their cable television. They've eliminated the passive, mindless entertainment that takes a toll on their time. They decided to use the Internet to select quality programs that satisfy curiosity or allow them to learn something new and improve the mind.

I'm not suggesting cancelling cable – I haven't done that yet - but I have started to make a list of programs and hours watched and make an assessment of how much time it takes away from focusing on what adds value to my life. As you make this assessment, carve time out of passive entertainment to take time for you and either walk, meditate or simply reflect on your journey. You'll discover significant extra time for personal growth.

Leave your comfort zone
Make an intention to do something that takes you out of your comfort zone, that scares you or makes you feel strange. Making an intention creates the sense that you own your day. It's easy to feel that other people drive your life when, in fact, you are the only one who has the ability to make that choice.

I do a headstand every day to remind myself that I can be brave, that I'm in control of my mind/body and spirit and willing to leave my comfort zone.

Take on challenges

Learn to live skillfully by choosing to take on challenges that are meaningful. Challenges can be small, medium or large, but no matter the size, they are all significant. Meeting challenges directly without equivocation gives you the opportunity to get to know yourself better and to claim more time for personal growth.

Shift your mindset

Your life is truly important, a gift that needs to be cherished and honored. It's difficult to make time in your life without examining or breaking old patterns of organization, control issues and limiting beliefs that take time away from adding value to your life. Change your mindset and be surprised by the results. Decide what you really want in life. Everybody secretly wants to love, to have confidence, respectability, and excitement. Why would you want to compromise these values by mindless entrapments that limit your ability to create time to accomplish your dreams and desires?

Taking time for you is a choice and a practice. It is undoubtedly one of the most important gifts you can give yourself. Time adds value to your life and enhances your happiness.

HERE'S TO THE LADIES WHO LUNCH
So here's to the girls on the go--
Everybody tries.
Look into their eyes,
And you'll see what they know.
- From *Here's To The Ladies Who Lunch* by Stephen Sondheim,
Company

REFRAME THE AGING PROCESS – YOU SEXY THING

The ageless Cher is turning 68. She recently was seen attending the Met Gala in New York City. The theme of this year's gala was everything Chinese and those in attendance wore costumes to reflect an aspect of the museum's exhibition. Cher wore a long gown of blended vivid dark colors with less vamp than in previous decades. The only alluring factor was a risky décolletage.

There are certainly aspects to aging that require reframing as each decade passes. I assume Cher was reframing at the Met Gala this year. Cher is still very much Cher and she saw no need to compete with Lady Gaga.

I just took a road trip with my best friend from grammar school and as we explored a few wineries in the Napa Valley, we were reminded of how our personalities, rhythms and energy have changed very little since we were young. Yet, we reflected that we couldn't drink as much wine as we thought, we looked more forward to reading before bed than gathering at a local pub, and we ate less. Still, we had energy to spare.

Recognizing that you are undergoing subtle changes in the aging process requires less literal thought and more mindful awareness. Reframe aging with subtlety and grace.

Take Care of Yourself, Not Just Others
It is an axiom that women are the caretakers of the world. People, organizations and places that give gratitude for your help make you feel good. But as you age, the way you take care of *yourself* matters more. You need more breathing space and more time to self-reflect.

It's perfectly awesome to give yourself many gifts throughout the day, the week and the month: practice yoga, meditate, play a round of golf, read, learn something new, or take a relaxing bath. It's not just fun, but doing things for yourself also plays a huge role in controlling stressors in your environment. As you reframe aging, remember that you are the most important gift you have.

Set Boundaries in Personal and Professional Relationships
From the time you entered adulthood, you heard the caution: set boundaries with family, friends and career. As you age, there may be a growing or extended family that requires your attention. You might have friends who need your companionship or your resources.

Yet part of reframing age is to note that time is precious and the mantra to *honor your body, mind and spirit* takes precedence. Listen to your needs and desires and be aware when *no* is the appropriate response.

Face Life's Challenges and Changes Joyfully
You've lived many decades. You are one of the fortunate people. Most of the struggle has passed and you are living a freer life. Yet you still encounter challenges and changes, moving to another city or traveling might be uncomfortable or cumbersome.

As you age, there is a need to reframe your needs and desires and to leave your comfort zone out of necessity or to reconfigure your life. Be ready, alert and conscious so that you will manage these changes with joy and positive energy.

Learn from Your Mistakes, Forgive Yourself and Move On
We all make mistakes and it is often said that it is more difficult to forgive yourself for your mistakes than to forgive others who injure you. Forgiveness is about surrendering, accepting and moving forward.

If you get sucked into the vortex of the unforgiving mindset, you risk losing clarity of thought, clear communication and empathy. As you reframe aging, practicing a generosity of spirit that will make life more joyful and productive.

Learn to Develop a Greater Sense of Personal Awareness: Stay Present
As you age, past memories can seem more important than the present. It's easy to be drawn into memory, but it is mentally more productive and exciting to be mindful of your environment, the people who surround you and the opportunities that are in front of you today.

Living a healthy and well-balanced life is your legacy. It is an accomplishment and an acknowledgement that you are still unleashing and reframing your personal power and professional integrity as you age.

I had an experience 10 years ago that I'm reminded of every time I go into a department store. My best friend and I were at the makeup counter and no one came to wait on us.

"It's our age," she said to me with disdain.

"Our age? We're not even 60 yet," I quipped.

"You're clueless," she replied. "We're not getting waited on because they can't see us. We're getting older. We're invisible."

"That's ridiculous. We look hot and hip and we're trying to buy some age-defying makeup." I laughed. "It's not about age. They need our business."

"No, really. They can't see us," she said firmly.

"Get over it, Arlene. The sales lady is at the cash register. That's why she can't wait on us."

My friend didn't realize that being seen has nothing to do with aging. Being seen is all about attitude and exuding confidence and style. Being seen is about understanding that women are more beautiful and certainly more interesting as they get older.

Most of my friends are young – really young – and they actually find me interesting. I guess at 70 plus I've got some pearls of wisdom gleaned from years of experience. Or maybe as my friend said to me on the occasion of my 70th birthday, "So far so good."

Life gets better as you age because you are more mindful about your place in the universe. You have a greater ability to recognize amazing possibilities and imagine untold opportunities. Simple things take on new importance. You can say "NO" without guilt and "YES" with more joy. You can find humor in almost anything because you finally understand irony.

Here's the best part of aging with mindfulness: You can let go of the past, get rid of emotional baggage, be present, look forward with excitement, and forgive anybody who ever said an unkind word to you because it's in the past, it's over, no más! It's a relief to know that you no longer have to "prove" you are worthy of being you.

Aging is like being in recovery, but a lot more fun.

According to the UCLA Mindful Awareness Center, the practice of mindfulness alters the molecular structure of the brain and makes you healthier and a whole lot happier. When a practice of mindfulness is at the center of your aging journey, you resonate a state of peace, increase personal awareness, foster great health and inspire growth and transformation.

Being invisible because of age is a myth perpetuated by those who feel badly about aging. We need to empower ourselves and be mindful that the aging process is a gift, not an excuse to throw a pity party. That's not a party you want to attend.

I've been a puppet, a pauper, a pirate, a poet, a pawn and a king
I've been up and down and over and out and I know one thing
Each time I find myself flat on my face
I pick myself up and get back in the race.
- From *That's Life* as sung by Frank Sinatra

GET RID OF YOUR EMOTIONAL BAGGAGE, DUDE

Zeus:

The Greek god Zeus is a prominent patron of June because he is an archetype of light, clarity, power and strength – all themes found in the month of June. Zeus is also a symbol of summer. Known as the "father of the gods," Zeus is also a figure for Father's Day, a U.S. holiday held in June.

June is also a month of balance, and it can't very well feature a father god, Zeus, without a mother goddess. Danu is considered the ultimate mother in Celtic wisdom. In fact, she was responsible for establishing a whole tribe of people (Tuatha De Danann) in Ireland. Danu is the epitome of artful class, craftsmanship and devotion to creative expression.

Let's put these ideas together and see what we can deduce: Light, power, and strength verses balance, wisdom, and creativity. These expressions seem perfectly suited to examine our own emotional baggage.

How much does your emotional baggage weigh? A lot? Not much? You don't have any? Oh, come on! Everyone carries around leftover negative emotions from the past, a suitcase full of blame and finger pointing, jealousies, feelings of failure and toxic relationships. We probably have enough emotional baggage to last several lifetimes.

Have you noticed how you feel strong after you have been in the light? When you open yourselves up to the light, you find clarity. With clarity comes power and engagement.

Every day I find the need to get away from my computer and walk outside into the light and just stand there in absolute joy. Lately, I've been going swimming at my client's home after we do yoga or walk the hills. The light helps release my negative emotions, the shame of my failed relationships, and the guilt of not doing enough for my family. The light creates clarity of emotion, and I release negativity as I experience strength.

Emotional baggage is a metaphorical image of carrying all the disappointments, wrongs, and trauma of the past around with us. That kind of baggage can be a heavy load. How can we lighten it?

Danu was a powerful woman who created her life rather than let life take control of her. When things were not going the way she wanted them to, she established her own tribe with a fair and balanced infrastructure. Danu was an artfully skilled self-manager who probably (I'm surmising here) was not derailed by negative people or toxic situations. She, too, followed the light in the month of June and became stronger and richer for her truthful choices.

A QUICK WAY TO STAY POSITIVE WHEN YOU'VE GOT THE BLUES

We all like to think of ourselves as the woman warrior, the indomitable female, the can-do girl, or the hunter gatherer/protector of those we love, the man who is responsible for family. No matter the gender we hope to live every moment with intensity and attention.

But, alas, we are human and we have our down days, up days and in-between days. We have days when we don't feel as positive or as motivated and days when our energy gets stuck and the balance tips toward the negative.

The pull of the couch, the lure of mindless entertainment, the distraction of people, places and things drain the potential for positive energy. Hopefully, we don't have too many of the down days when sitting on the couch sounds more appealing than going for a walk.

Perhaps the overwhelming nature of a large project prevents you from taking the first step, so you decide to "start tomorrow." Maybe it's more of an abstract lack of motivation. You feel unable to focus on what needs to be done or what you want to do for fun. You can't seem to get there.

The key to staying positive when you're feeling down is the ability to consciously focus attention on your state of being emotionally, physically, intellectually, and spiritually. Your ability to focus on yourself – to self-reflect – requires you to let go of the mindless messages, the energy drains and attachments from your environment. Sometimes technology is your worst enemy.

The total of your distractions has a negative effect on how you feel. Curing the negative effect is not a skill like being organized or having massive amounts of self-control. Moving from the negative to the positive and lifting yourself out of the blues is all about changing your mindset and discovering new mindsets that reframe your attitude.

Let's look at an example of turning the negative into a positive:

You are fixed to the couch mindlessly watching yet another mundane TV program. The day is passing quickly and you feel like a sloth. Turn off the TV, close your eyes and take a few minutes to breathe deeply. Draw the attention into yourself and experience the present moment *without judging or labeling*. Your head will begin to clear of distraction and clutter, your resistance will begin to subside and the negative energy will turn into positive energy.

Then get off the couch and turn yourself upside down – into a forward standing bend. The inversion stimulates the neurotransmitters and a flood of energy goes through your body emitting adrenalin, serotonin, dopamine and norepinephrine. Do some stretching, take a walk, or go to the gym and get even more energized. It's a startling transformation!

We all get into the habit of labeling and judging our actions and thoughts. Labeling and judging can create a state of resistance that is toxic and negative. Staying positive gives you the courage to say *Yes* instead of *No* when you feel immobilized. It is then that you can release your personal power and find direction and fulfillment.

DON'T SETTLE FOR LESS: DINE ON CAVIAR

A few weeks ago, the *New York Times* had an interview with Gloria Steinem on the occasion of her 80th birthday. When asked if she had any regrets, she said, "It's not that I would do anything different. It's that I'd do things faster."

When Ms. Steinem, one of my role models, candidly wished she would have gotten to where she was going in life a little faster, she was referring specifically to writing a book she had planned to do for decades and just never got around to until recently. It seemed Ms. Steinem was a procrastinator, but who isn't?

But Gloria Steinem at 80 years old still travels and speaks on issues she is passionate about and she's making tracks, making up for lost time. She's not exactly hurrying to the end of her life, it's more like she's making the most of her life and she is, metaphorically speaking, gorging on caviar at the moment. I doubt that this female icon ever tasted dirt.

Don't eat dirt when you can gorge on caviar and live a full and rich life. Eating dirt tastes terrible and has no nutritional value. In some circles, it might be considered maintenance food. A diet of empty carbs with lots of sugar and too much flour is going to slow your brain down, impair your senses and inhibit a focused mind/body connection. Food with no substance limits your creative imagination.

Aspire to something more substantial – a diet that honors your body and mind. I know that I don't get all the great food nutrients that I need for the day so I make a green drink. It was off-putting at first because of the earthy smell and powerful green taste. I used to hold my breath and think of a delicious Mexican dinner complete with a side of lard while it went down, but I'm used to it now – no sugar and no white flour. No more feel-good "dirt" for me! I've now gotten used to caviar and am grateful that the bad stuff is out of my system.

Moonlight In A Martini

Life is about the search – the search for a higher level of virtuosity. You've got plenty of abundance, all right, but doesn't it strike you that you can reach a little higher, be more fruitful and generous and cultivate an idea of a future that gives your gifts a whole new meaning? I want to see moonlight in my martini.

Rabbi Hillel (a famous Jewish religious leader who lived from 110 BCE to 7 CE) said, "If I am not for myself, who is for me? And when I am for myself, what am 'I'? And if not now, then when?"

Why would you choose to eat dirt? It's because the usual suspects inevitably show up – fear, doubt, regret and blame – and they become excuses not to live your life completely. Take off your lead boots and run quickly to the real feast where caviar abounds.

PUT ON YOUR RED SHOES AND DANCE

You feel safe in this moment. It feels nice and comfortable, but make no mistake, comfort is a trap.

So put on your red shoes and dance.

Your life may seem in order, you may feel you've got everything organized, but there is a rigid essence that paradoxically has no resemblance to a comfort zone.

So put on your red shoes and dance.

Comfort is not exciting. There's no forward movement. Your energetic spirit is sidelined. Life drags.

So put on your red shoes and dance.

Make plans to be the best that you can be. If you never articulate a vision, never picture something more creative in the future, you'll never rise higher than your circumstances.

So put on your red shoes and dance.

 Don't think your needs aren't enough to build a complete life. This is how the vision begins and current mindsets produce future possibilities.

 So put on your red shoes and dance.

Your life is a message to the world and sharing it with others is important. That's a legacy – the ability to give to others and to the society at large lives long after you leave the earth.

 So put on your red shoes and dance.

Be brave in your choices and make the most of what you have.

 This is the simple truth: Life's a two-fold proposition – to be truly great is to be of service to others as well as yourself. So dance with your vision of an exciting and abundant life day by day and watch how beautifully your life unfolds.

 Get up everyday and *deeply desire* that vision. Put yourself in the center of the world you want to live in and please, dedicate yourself to what truly counts.

THINGS YOU SHOULD KNOW BEFORE YOU GET YOUR FIRST TATTOO

I got my first tattoo while living in Venice, California, in 1996. I was 53 years old, long before Baby Boomers had an inkling that tattoos were not just for bikers

 Several years prior to living in Venice, I had a breast biopsy that revealed a fibroid tumor. My internist told me it was probably benign, and it was, but it measured about 3 centimeters. I named it Gus.

Instead of suturing the area, the doctor used staples and they left permanent scarring. It looked like needle marks. Every time I wore something with a low cut neckline, you could see scar tissue and the indentation at the top of my right breast. Not a good look.

In the Heart of Venice

It occurred to me that I could cover the scars and minimize the ski slope appearance by getting a tattoo. I met an attractive and inspirational Australian who created a design of a rose on a vine that linked the staples in a beautiful artistic way.

By the time I was 60, I decided the tattoo wasn't finished and consulted a very famous tattoo artist in Los Angeles who suggested another rose and vine to complete the landscape. I asked Zulu to give me the symbol of OM somewhere below my belly button. In the meantime, my younger son was home from college, saw my first tattoo, and had a conniption fit right on the beach at Malibu. "How could you, Mom?"

Since then, I've gotten another tattoo to compliment my OM – a sacred lotus flower in neon orange and yellow also below my belly button. I had just broken up with my last boyfriend and was feeling liberated and frisky.

Tattoo Nation

Today tattoos are ubiquitous. In Austin practically everyone but uptight squares are into tattoos. Entire bodies are covered with "ink," even my best girl buddies now in their 60s are embracing the trend.

One of my male friends didn't understand the concept of tattooing and declared he would never, ever date a girl with a tattoo – that limits the female population in Austin for sure. He asked me why I got tattoos. Translated: how did I get up the nerve to do such a far-out, ridiculous thing? I didn't tell him I'm ready to get another one at almost 70. It seems a fitting birthday present to myself.

In the event someone else asks me the same thing and looks at me like I wear the "Scarlet A", I compiled a list of 5 things you should have mentally locked down before you enter a tattoo parlor:

1 You've got to trust someone.
It might as well be your tattoo artist. He's probably more trust-worthy than your ex-boyfriend or maybe even your brother. It all starts with a belief – a belief in someone who can honor your wishes completely, communicate with you clearly and create his version of your version of artistry even for a brief 2 to 3 hours.

2 It's a confidence builder.
Some people thought I was crazy, some thought I was brave and some thought my tattoo was to give my sons and brother a shock. Maybe it's all three, but it's my statement of who I am in solidarity with others who have had the confidence to be true to themselves.

3 It will change your perspective about your body.
Most people have body-image problems. We think we're too fat, too skinny, or not proportioned properly. But no matter how you feel about your body, it's your body so take pride in it! It's yours to do what you want so dare to make a statement and it might change how you feel about your body. Embrace the change and be delighted.

4 It's a way to keep building your wins.
Getting a tattoo is your achievement. You don't have to compare

your artistry with others because your individual and special tattoo signifies your ability to take yourself out of your comfort zone and do things that are brave. It's an achievement of wins that will always be visible.

5 You are joining a tribe as old as mankind.
Tattooing is as old as mankind, dating back to almost the Neolithic times. Tattoos can symbolize identity, manifest a philosophy, and make a tribal statement of purpose. You get a tattoo and you become part of a tribe that bears witness to the history of man. It may be a tribe of one or of many, but your artistic ink says you are proud of your bravery, courage and individualism.

My tattoos remind me of who I am and what I'm proud of – that I'm giving my best in life, I didn't hold back and I'm focused on my achievements with my rebel sense of self.

MODIFY YOUR YOGA PRACTICE AS YOU AGE

I had an epiphany more than a year ago concerning my yoga practice. I was teaching one of my many yoga flow classes during the week, still in great health and physical shape for 70 and thinking how grateful I was that I didn't have any physical issues.

Then suddenly, out of nowhere, I had a moment of panic as I descended from plank pose into chaturanga. I couldn't hold my body above the floor and move into updog because my right arm and shoulder collapsed. My chest hit the floor with a thud. The pain was palpable.

I casually dismissed it with, "I'm having an off day. My right shoulder must be more sore than usual, I'll return to my perfect practice tomorrow. I'm the queen of chaturanga to updog and nothing can stop me after 20 years of practice."

Limited arm and shoulder movement persisted accompanied by daily pain. Although I tried to ignore it, the reality was that I was going to have to modify my practice and consult an orthopedic surgeon.

An Athlete's Journey

"Twenty years of yoga and a lifetime of athletic endeavor have caught up with you, Joan," my orthopedic surgeon told me as he looked at my MRI results. "You've had a long run."

"Don't put me out to pasture yet, Doc. I'm not finished," I said.

"I see lots of people come through my office with the same injury," the doctor said. "It's common with athletes. It starts with arthritis between your shoulder blades in the supraspinatus muscle. Your supraspinatus tendon is torn in several places and your have tendonitis in the rotator cuff. You also have an impinged bicep tendon and your arm has limited range of motion."

Just shoot me, I thought. They shoot horses, don't they?

I was always attracted to a *yin* yoga practice, a deeply meditative and reflective practice in which floor-based postures are held for extended periods of time. However, I also liked my dynamic *yang* practice because my muscles were strengthened by repetitive motion. It seemed that my injury was going to be a blessing in disguise; it gave me impetus to explore the practice of *yin* yoga as an alternative to *yang*.

Here are five ways I mindfully modified a vigorous 20-year yoga practice to keep my mind, body and spirit fully integrated and bring me less physical stress with more of the same joy:

More Yin Stretching

When I practice or teach yoga, I always begin by stretching. Muscles need to be warm to function effectively. Previously, my stretching usually involved about 5-7 minutes of cross-legged forward bends, stretching with arms overhead, a twist in both directions and side bends.

I've now extended the stretching period to 12-15 minutes and include an extended forward standing bend with arms over head and some knee flexes from side to side. I find that my flexibility has increased over the past year. Score one for injuries.

More Restorative Postures

Bringing the body to balance and flexibility is a benefit of any yoga practice, however, an extended focus on restorative yoga postures is a grounding and calming experience. It's a way to let go of mind clutter and to fully decompress from a stressful day. Putting my legs up the wall is my favorite posture to fully open my heart and pay more attention to my breath. Child's pose is another way to be fully present to your mind, body and spirit.

More Neck Rolls

Neck rolls sound simple, right? You may think it's kind of an okay thing to do in yoga, but the neck roll movement is very important to the base of our neck, upper back, shoulders and to the all around line of our spine.

One intention in yoga is to keep the neck vertebrae in line with the vertebrae of the spine, which forms a straight line from the crown of the head down to the lumber and sacrum. Now that I spend more time with head rolls rather than glossing through them, I find that they have a direct correlation to more perfect sitting and walking postures.

More Knee Work in Chaturanga

The days of letting my body down to the floor in plank pose without using my knees is over. Although I have achieved more muscle flexibility with physical therapy and the impingement of the bicep muscle is decreasing, I am not attempting to push my body into a position that it doesn't want to go. I put my knees down on the floor first and put less weight on my back, shoulder and arms as I let myself down to my mat. I still strengthen all the muscles involved in the upper back and arms, but without the added physical stress.

More Time in Resting Pose

In the past I occasionally cut time from the last pose in a yoga practice, even though I was taught that resting pose is the most important posture in a yoga practice. I would get antsy because I had to be somewhere – where I don't know. With a more meditative and purposeful yoga practice, I mindfully respect the benefits of letting go and gaining acceptance as I end my practice.

As I adjusted my yoga practice during the last year to reflect my physical limitations, that adjustment has brought acceptance, surrender, joy and more mindfulness to my practice. In fact, my physical injury has taught me more about the meaning of yoga than I could possibly imagine. I no longer hold on to the *perfect*. I am simply grateful that I have so much mobility at 72. Like life, a yoga practice is constantly and perfectly in transition.

LONGEVITY IS YOUR BEST FRIEND

You've heard it before and it is a true axiom: *You get better as you age.*

I want to put it out there in the universe: I like getting older. I like staying sexy, smart and strong at my age.

Longevity gives you the opportunity to increase your value and competence.

Here's what you have to look forward to as you age:

You'll enjoy a more expansive sense of time and place.
Your time is your own. You may have responsibilities to family and friends, but most of the time you determine when and where. Of course, if you are taking care of elderly parent(s), you have certain rituals to follow, but with daily planning for time commitments and family responsibilities, you can fulfill your intentions with care and attention. You can then make the most of your downtime by doing what you love most: exercising, cooking, dancing, reading or other things that bring you joy.

You'll find joy in your state of awareness.
The majority of people fail to look inside themselves for answers to their deepest issues. Self-awareness is continually being compromised by distractions – people, places and things get in the way of your happiness and clear intentions.

As you age, self-reflection is not a luxury but it is a necessity. Longevity means you can say good-bye to your physical aches and pains and get connected to the positive energy that surrounds mind, body and spirit. Then you can walk the path of mindfulness giving you a higher level of consciousness and awareness of what adds value to your life.

You'll have the opportunity to be a mentor and role model for others.
Longevity has given you resources and perceptions that others recognize. You are more willing to discuss age-related changes (especially those related to sexuality), you have wisdom when talking to those who need advice about making changes in life

or in work and you have the ability to feel deep empathy for the suffering of others.

You'll get smarter.
Longevity has allowed you to unleash the intellectual and emotional power of self-knowledge. You see yourself as the actual person you are, always ready, willing and wiser.

You are someone who is sexy, smart and strong. You are someone who lives by a stronger standard, someone who believes in yourself and someone who can be counted on by the people that matter to you. You are the boss of you.

PART 2
Stay Smart

Before I began this book, I laid in bed for months in the early morning hours thinking about what I should call it. I'm direct and mildly confrontational so I entertained *Get Out Of Bed Every Day and Kick Butt*, however, it might be construed as a military manual for staying buff. Other musings brought: *Get Up Every Day and Show Up*, and yet those are the intentions behind the actual title of this book. No one is the boss of you *except you – kick butt and show up.*

Miguel Cervantes gives a nicer, cleaner take on showing up for your life:

Make it thy business to know thyself, which is the most difficult challenge in life.

That challenge begins with a conscious intention to connect your mind, body and spirit into an integrated, well-balanced individual with unlimited potential for personal and professional success.

Enter Barbara Stanwych

My mother was a whiz at making a success out of everything. She even made scrambled eggs on a meatless Friday nights taste like caviar. She knew who she was and how to make money from her talents. She taught me the same lesson when I was in high school.

As a junior in high school in 1963, I was a public speaking whiz kid. I even made money on the speaking circuit: Lions Club International, Native Sons of the Golden West and the American Legion. My mother saw to it that I used my speaking talents to the best of my abilities. To ensure I would win scholarship money for college, she helped me write my speeches all the while sitting at her sewing machine creating the latest fashionista outfit. She was hemming my prom dress while I stood three feet on a platform built especially for me.

"Stay still, Joanie until I tell you to move," she barked at me.

"Mom, I'm stuck on my Lion Club speech. I need help, not a hem."

"I've got an idea. The speech you are working on is about challenges in the world," she said. "Let's start by finding a quote. That's always a great way to get inspiration."

Mom went to *Bartlett's Book of Quotations* and looked up challenges. There it was – Miguel Cervantes telling us that the first challenge in life is to know yourself.

If you know yourself, you have the ability to self-reflect and self-reflection can bring you to balance and bliss.

The inspiration from that quote set my speech on a winning path. Of course, the latest fashion I wore on stage sewn from her incredible hands made me a star.

Know yourself/know your talents. I still use that same quote in my speeches today.

Hang Out With Yourself

I don't know about you, but I like to hang out with myself. I attribute that ability to six decades of trying to understand who I am, what makes me tick, what are my proclivities, my good attributes, my lack of clarity, what triggers my anger, where my ego needs to reside and myriad other special considerations that keep me emotionally, psychologically, intellectually and physically balanced.

I like myself even better as I age because I have more self knowledge. It's amazing how spending time with myself without myriad distractions in my environment increases my ability to self-reflect. Self-reflection is a practice that reduces stress and anxiety and leads to a happier sense of self.

When I feel a total sense of well being, my level of consciousness is awesome. I'm not just focusing better, I am feeling better. I'm not parceling out my life in bits and pieces, and I'm not being thrust hither and yon. I am much more mindful of thoughts, emotions, desires, and feelings and I find stillness in the midst of my humanness.

As a yoga teacher I advocate a daily 10-minute meditation practice. Meditation is a powerful tool that will open the mind, define your needs and certainties, find significant connections with others, provide positive energy and make room for surprises. This holistic approach brings a more relaxed, balanced, happy and loving mindset.

Exercise and Be Smarter

Did you know that you could *optimize mind wellness by pairing it with physical exercise*: walking, running, hiking, biking, yoga (my favorite), and the ever-expanding workout routines that are combining the mind/body connection?

Exercise also increases problem-solving skills by bridging the right/left brain to get rid of mental blocks.

Don't Dumb Down Your Life

When you are scattered and just trying to get through the day, you're not smart. You let distractions get in the way of clear thinking. Your brain isn't functioning on the highest level with clear focus and intention. Your thinking gets small and the size of your thinking determines the size of your results.

Staying smart means choosing balance, judging your surroundings, deciding on what works best for you and remaining in a place of mental emotional and psychological stability.

Balancing work and life is not just "food-for-thought," nor is it about stasis and symmetry. Balance is the practice of being flexible and having the ability to change. There are countless advantages to having a balanced life and looking after yourself in every aspect of mind, body and spirit. It's an awesome experience to be the boss of you and discover the truth of who you are.

Consider Stretching Your Mind

Did you know it's possible to stretch your mind at any age? You can actually get smarter, retain more information, make better decisions and keep your mind and body in top condition throughout your life.

If my mother had bought into the idea of *aging diminishes the human condition,* she wouldn't have accomplished half of what she did in her lifetime. In her mid-70s she created a senior aerobics video she sold to her classes at the Senior Center and at the Country Club in her community. It was a huge hit!

At 78, my mother was crowned Miss Senior Citizen of Las Vegas. Her talent was a fashion show she put on the main stage of the Rivera Hotel. In all of about 4 minutes, my mother changed her clothes on stage in front of a packed house. It was amazing! My mother was just getting started on her 8th decade. She continued to teach senior aerobics and serve 2 terms as president of the women's club. The ladies wouldn't let her go.

You don't have to buy into myths that aging diminishes your brain capacity:

Age makes your brain tired

You get dimmer with age

It takes longer to process information as you get older

Too much background noise interferes with thinking

It takes longer to understand something

One of the most exciting areas of scientific study today is the study of the brain. UCLA has one of the most famous brain mapping centers in the world. In the hallowed offices at the UCLA Brain Mapping Center, scientists and researchers advance the understanding of the relationship between structure and function in the brain. They research how the brain records new information as well as the brain's ability to learn.

The most exciting discovery is that the brain has a natural ability to remodel itself through life. This quality is known as *plasticity*. The brain is not static, but always changing, and hopefully, always in the direction of a positive quality of life. When you know that the brain has this capacity, you might rethink how vital and important it is to keep your brain functioning at its upmost capacity.

Of course, Alzheimer's disease will adversely affect the natural trajectory of your brain; however, always using your brain to its fullest capacity and maintaining functionality under normal conditions often negates the onset of dementia.

One of the best ways to keep your brain sharp is to pay attention to your senses: eyes, ears, taste, touch, smell. Memories are made up of what you sense. The brain processes sensory information and uses this information to construct your experiences – from great moments in your life to the mundane. Later in my mother's life, I can remember her writing down everything – all lists, all-important information, including emotional observations, which helped to keep her brain sharp to the end.

How do you make memories and store that information in the brain? You have millions and millions of neurons in the brain.

These neurons increase your brain stamina. You can lose thousands of neurons daily so you have to work harder to stop neurons from dying. It's like running a marathon to keep your brain functioning, but you can do it with mindfulness – staying 100% present.

If you don't take care of your brain by exercising it, you'll develop what's called a fuzzy brain. That's when mistakes are made in the most elemental operations due to a lack of clear thinking – and then, of course, all of the brain's higher operations in thinking and behaving will suffer. A brain won't improve if it's operating with incomplete information and poor logic.

How many times have you lost your keys – house or car – in the last month? I'm a master at losing my keys. Three or four times a week I misplace them. I do the same thing with my reading glasses. Most of the time this happens, my brain is detached from my body. I am not present in my environment and my brain is some place else.

But even if I am not rushing around to leave the house or get on a plane, I have found myself in what I call an "out of body experience" where I mentally go some place else, but my body stays where it was. I've detached from time and place as we all do. That's kind of a scary place to be.

If you understand the premise that the brain has plasticity and continually learns throughout life, you will be able to reframe mindsets and thought patterns and think yourself to optimal health and happiness. You'll also be able to judge the role of past references and experiences in relation to the present focus, thereby expanding your mental acuity. This learning optimization eliminates roadblocks to future thought and creativity. Every part of your life will flourish: personal, relationship, and business.

You will:

Focus Your Attention with Ease

Increase Your Brain Speed

Improve Your Memory

Enhance People Skills

Sharpen Your Intelligence

Tune up Your Navigation

I used to be hopeless with directions. I was saved by Google Maps and Siri and they make my life so much easier and happier. I'm less frustrated and drive without stress most of the time.

Yet that's no excuse for not paying attention to the above list. When I drive, my senses are operating efficiently; my brain speed is increased because I'm using it in real time. I'm memorizing landmarks, street names, and other signs that I'm on the right road. I'm completely focused on my environment and my navigational skills get better each time out. In fact, sometimes I test myself when I get back in the car by not using Siri or Google Maps to see how well I paid attention getting to my original destination.

When I'm completely lost due to Google Maps incompetence and Siri's inability to comprehend what I'm saying, I strengthen my people skills at the food mart at the closest gas station I can find. I'm good to go with my visual memory in gear.

Staying smart is easy: Simply *be responsive to your amazing presence.*

YOU ARE WHAT YOU THINK

Eleanor Roosevelt said: "Great minds discuss ideas, average minds discuss events, and small minds discuss people."

Have you ever considered how much time you spend on the phone talking about other people, at your computer writing gossipy emails, dishing dirt over lunch with your friends, or spending time at social events and happy hours talking about what couples are divorcing?

The truth is harsh: Engaging in mindless conversation about people you know or don't know uses up brain space, leaving less cognitive ability for Eleanor Roosevelt's declaration that "great minds discuss ideas."

Idle chitchat adds nothing significant to life and just wastes energy and time. A continual diet of mundane conversation keeps you unproductive and less inclined to make changes or create a more appealing and joyful state of mind. Being seduced by other people's lives isn't the most elegant of places to be.

As I have aged, I've lost patience to entertain long conversations about other people, their problems and personal issues. With the exception of medical issues concerning family and friends, I try not to engage in mindless conversation. I prefer to focus on good news, writing, dancing and having fun outdoors.

You are what you think, and what you think determines the quality of your life. In fact, it just might be the definition of living life.

So, how do we get closer to a healthy state of being? The following are a few suggestions:

Bring More Mindfulness Into Your Life: Start a Meditation Practice
Meditation is a practice that focuses on staying present. When we talk about other people, speak about things that have already happened or conjecture about what might happen in the future, we miss out on the benefits of mindfulness: knowledge, present assessment of needs, clear thinking and communication and peaceful participation in debate, When mindfulness is present, you'll find you don't want to engage in conversation that produces no discernable result. It might even give you a newfound appreciation for silence.

Be More Project Oriented
Create, design, organize, volunteer with your positive energy and knowledge and give yourself and others gifts of love and gratitude. You won't be as inclined to talk endlessly to people who continually waste your time. It's unfortunate that most people are content with mindless conversations that distract you from your own well being and trap you into a one-sided relationship where you are only there for them. They don't need you as much as you think. Let them call someone else.

Be More Positive About Others
On several occasions, I have caught myself speaking negatively about others and was brought up short by how badly I felt after

the words came out of my mouth. Engaging in conversation that leads to negative outcomes changes your moods, affects your feelings and, by proxy, your health. Keep your brain filled with the fullness of life. You'll get rid of the "people hangover" and smile more.

Sometimes distraction is good, necessary and nearly unavoidable. However, the key is to be mindful of distractions and acknowledge when your behavior borders on addiction to the needs of others rather than honoring who you want to be. When this happens, make intentions to veer away from further attachments and free yourself to be yourself.

STRETCH YOUR MIND AT ANY AGE

Can you really stretch your mind to achieve more out of life? *Yes, absolutely, Yes*!

Mind stretching is the next revolution in personal development. I call this movement *The Rubberband Revolution* – the process of teaching the brain a new way of thinking by connecting the right/left brain more, thus, increasing the ability to problem solve. Stretching the mind enhances innovation and productivity, optimizes the way the mind functions and alleviates mental blocks.

Expanding your mental processes initiates the flow of limitless thought and unending possibilities. As a result, your personal and professional lives flourish and your general well-being is enhanced.

Most of us underuse our brains and confine ourselves to limited experiences. We naturally gravitate toward the past and confine our thoughts in the present to reside in our comfort zone. We resist any line of thinking that requires us to go deeper into solving problems or personal issues. Without realizing it, we have programmed ourselves not to stretch.

Yet, it's possible to reframe your thought patterns and negative mindsets and think yourself to optimal health and happiness.

An effective way to begin the process of stretching the mind is to examine some of your old mindsets, rigid ideas and limited perceptions that have dominated your thinking and lead to dead ends. A closed mind is dangerous because it allows you to compartmentalize and ignore uncomfortable thoughts and feelings. That's a prescription for mindless repetition and repetition can be a real brain killer.

Here are my 7 tips to stretch your mind at any age. I call them *Joan's Mind Fuel Tools for Life Renewal.*

1 *Reduce resistance*
   Your brain feels like it's sinking in quicksand. Why? It's called resistance and it's the most toxic force on the planet. It stops personal growth and creativity. You don't even know it's happening because it's human nature to resist. Resistance defies logic and that's dangerous. It takes away your potential for happiness, crushes your spirit and makes you less than you were born to be.

   Get conscious about what you are thinking and doing in life. Stay in the present. Ask: What do I need? When do I need it? How do I get it? Wake up every morning and make an intention to do the most important thing – something that brings you joy, gives positive energy, fulfills a need and lights your fire. Be aware and be clear about naming your needs every day so you can pursue your passions and your dreams.

2 *Have An Attitude of Gratitude*
   Gratitude starts your day with abundance. Name your gifts, and more importantly, name the gift you cannot live without. It's

important to be grateful even for negative experiences because they have the potential to become positive forces. Recently I saw a condo I wanted to buy, and before I knew it, it was sold and I was not happy. Soon after, I found a condo that suited me better and I was grateful. Did you know that having an attitude of gratitude changes the molecular structure of the brain and makes us healthier and happier?

3 *Eliminate Negative Self-Talk*
Negative self-talk is a completely mindless mental activity, mostly defensive and always toxic. It causes stress, anxiety and perpetuates past and future thinking. The power is in the now. Catch yourself in the moment of the negative thought and turn it into a positive! That takes practice, but you can do it!

4 *Be Vulnerable*
To be vulnerable is to have real strength. Getting in touch with your own emotional palette allows you to realize a more creative and fulfilling life. The path to self-reflection is embracing vulnerability. When you are emotionally open and honest, creativity takes hold, your imagination soars and you bring choice, strength and passion into your life.

5 *Learn To Adapt*
My mother taught me the way to learn to adapt is to understand that the only opinion worth anything comes from the truth inside of you. When you understand that premise, change comes from a strong conviction for action, coupled with confidence in your abilities and a willingness to cultivate curiosity. Don't label or judge the change. It's best to objectively observe change from a distance. When change happens, it energizes your imagination and reduces stress and anxiety.

6 *Find Your Passion*

Passion is an outpouring of positive energy for the ideas and interests that make a difference in your life. Ask yourself: What makes you come alive? What is your bliss? When you find happiness, you know your destiny. Believe me, life won't be any fun without having pursued your passion to the fullest because your passion is your life's adventure.

7 *Practice Forgiveness*

If we are honest, we know we have harbored resentments, collected injustices and become angry over insults that aren't that important. It's challenging and frustrating to forgive someone and it's even harder to forgive yourself. Forgiving is about letting go, surrendering and moving forward. Forgiving not only clears the mind of negativity, but also crucial in resolving issues, communicating effectively, providing empathy and living a happier life. Without forgiveness there would be no history, no hope and our species would have annihilated itself in endless retribution.

Stretching the mind includes taking some risks, a few leaps of faith and a willingness to make glorious mistakes. But the good news is there's no such thing as failure, there is only personal truth and it's always there for the taking.

MAGICAL THINKING

Ah, yes, the delicious state known as magical thinking, also known as daydreaming or fantasizing. Magical thinking is the storybook version of our life. We do it all the time because, well, it's fun and because we allow ourselves to fall into the unconscious state where we think the perfect happy life will show up on our doorstep.

Magical thinking happens frequently when we are in a situation that is uncomfortable and not to our liking. For example, we're in a relationship with a man or a woman that isn't working well, but we really want it to work out, so we pretend it is working out.

Voilà! Magical thinking. It never really works out because there is no truth to our magical thinking - it's all made up.

You daydream of a scene where a company gives you an opportunity to put everything you have worked so hard for into a position that reflects all your skills and talents. Your mind races to a future in which you shake the hand of your new boss and settle into the job of your dreams. Then the phone rings and suddenly you are taken out of your stupor when you are told the position no longer exists. A perfect made up moment.

I'm not sure we realize how frequently we steal time from ourselves by not relating to the truth of the moment. We lose time, energy and productivity. Why do we think everywhere else is better than the present?

Magical thinking can cause a whole lot of pain, heartbreak, lost dreams and lost time. It takes courage to live the truth every moment of the day. Magical thinking is the easy way out because our pictures are pretty and life is wonderful. But the truth is beautiful because it is also real.

Oh, you say sometimes reality is very difficult to deal with. Indeed it is, because it can feel as if it *shouldn't* be what it is. It should be the way you think it should be. Any other option produces angst.

Discomfort, pain and heartbreak are part of life. The practice of the Tao consists in daily losing. The Tao is our path of truth, and to keep true to ourselves it is important that we stay present and bear witness to our values.

If we stay mindful and present, if we give gratitude for our gifts and if we try to see our lives as what it is and not what we think should be, magical thinking will be kept at bay and saved for times of creativity and innovation.

One of my dearest friends queried me a few weeks ago in an email: "Franny," he wrote (that's his nickname for me), "I've got to take some lessons from you about changing. I can't seem to wrap my head around making a change in my living situation."

My friend's situation is quite unusual. He left Santa Fe, New Mexico, almost 20 years ago and took a job in Saudi Arabia to practice dentistry at Aramco, an oil company once owned by a conglomerate of several Western countries, including the U.S., with additional ownership by the Saudi government.

You're probably asking "why" my dentist friend took that job, but it made very good sense to him at the time. He is one of those citizens of the world and wanted to experience traveling to the most exotic places on earth.

My friend has had a wonderful, happy and peaceful life. He could leave Aramco any time to live elsewhere in the world and continue to pursue his passions, particularly music. Thus far, he has lead a complete life: he is a Buddhist a meditator, a tango dancer, a yogi and a man devoted to excellent physical and mental health.

But he can't quite come home – back to the good old USA – to the different realities of living in his home country. He's not quite sure he'll be as comfortable in another place. He hasn't surrendered to that idea. He hasn't let go yet.

"Fran. You gotta help me out. You love change. You move through life easily, and I'm having trouble with this one."

My answer to him was direct and forthright: "Well, my friend, twenty years is a heck of a long time in one place, in one culture, with unlimited free space, but your perspectives are limited and you've worn out all the emotional contexts. Time for change."

Changing mindsets is very challenging because the defensive brain cannot change. It's awash in stressor chemicals that cause the brain to go into survival mode accessing old behaviors regardless of their ineffectiveness.

How do we change our mentality? How do we reframe the old mindsets, the old mental categories, get rid of rigid ideas, self-important opinions and our preoccupation with goals instead of process? How do we eliminate this by-product of stress and anxiety that digs us deeper into a false sense of comfort? How do we let go of our fears and pursue our own truth?

Maybe my dentist friend has been slowly mentally creeping into the moment he will leave the cocoon and come home. In the meantime, fears pile up. What's on the other side? What if I hate where I end up?

Darling friend, forget the other side. What does the other side matter? Fears are manufactured, groundless and maybe even delusional, told to you by a universal language that lives in fear. My mother used to tell me not to fear anything because it's a waste of time. It's more fun to be surprised by life.

Year after year my friend said he was coming home "next year" and maybe now as the twenty-year mark rolls around the statute of limitations is kicking in. Who knows what is the trigger.

Sarah Silverman has a riff on change I love. A friend said to her, "I'm going to start my diet tomorrow." Sarah says bluntly, "No you're not." The friend is resentful. "What do you mean? I'm going on my diet tomorrow." Sarah replies, "No, you're not, no you're not, no you're not!!! Because if you were going on a diet you would already be on the diet instead of just telling me you're going on a diet!" I love human nature. We're so predictable.

The truth is that if we take on the challenge of change, we'll never burn out. Change energizes our imagination by reframing old mindsets, allowing us to see multiple perspectives in a variety of contexts increasing the possibilities that a new approach to an idea or situation will be discovered.

We can unleash the mental and emotional powers of self-reflection when we're deciding on change - every single bit of energy is directed towards positive growth and maybe even transformation. What we choose may not meet our needs in the moment, but on a continuum, change will always be positive if we listen to the truth inside of us.

Remember, fear will stop us from action, but fascination won't let us walk away.

Living skillfully is about making mindful decisions that enhance our life, deepen our ability to assess our individual needs and open up to limitless possibilities and opportunities. Leave superstition and dogma for the mindless. Please don't squander the privilege of consciousness because that's where the truth resides and bravery begins.

Postscript: My friend came back home to the states this month to reside in Austin where music is everywhere and energy abounds.

SUPERCALIFRAGILISTICEXPIALIDOCIOUS
Supercalifragilisticexpialidocious!
Even though the sound of it
Is something quite atrocious,
If you say it loud enough
You'll always sound precocious,
Supercalifragilisticexpialidocious!
- From *The Sound of Music*

YOUR BRAIN ROCKS!

Is our brain our mind or is our brain simply a part of our mind? Are they one and the same or different and separate entities, one tagged as neuroscience (the brain) and the other (the mind) pure vibrating energy?

Another way of looking at the mind is to think of it as the non-physical entity of our being. Scientists and philosophers argue that the mind does not exist without the brain. Brain and mind are both the rocket and fuel of the human being. They are yoked, inextricably connected to each other by the body.

The mind conducts "thought" faster than the speed of light and retains all experience whether consciously or not. The mind creates, projects and receives thoughts. It expresses emotions and feelings and it determines the positive or negative levels in our bodies. However, most of all, the mind is associated with consciousness, and that being true, the mind can stretch because our consciousness can expand!

The mind always wants to get to know itself better.

The yogic philosopher Patanjali told us that: "*When you are inspired by some great purpose, some extraordinary project, and all your thoughts break their bonds: Your mind transcends limitations, your consciousness expands in every direction, and you find yourself in a new, great, and wonderful world. Dormant forces, faculties and talents become alive, and you discover yourself to be a greater person by far than you ever dreamed yourself to be."*

Mahatma Ghandi told us: "*You can chain me, you can torture me, you can even destroy this body, but you will never imprison my mind.*"

None of us tap into our brain 100% of the time. Most or maybe half is unused during the day. What if you expanded your mental processes and could initiate the flow of limitless thought and possibilities? Your personal and work life, relationships and happiness quotient would flourish.

Your brain can get lazy and willful without your awareness. However, making a conscious intention to be mindful of your essential values in life – those that you live by – stability, resilience and balance – allows you to stretch the mind more frequently, providing you with clear thinking, better communication and well-defined relationships.

Stay conscious and use your mind: It's free and a measurable indicator of how joyful your path in life can be.

SLEEP DEPRIVED BUT STAYING ALIVE

You know how something sounds like a good idea, and then it's not?

That happened to me last week when I joined a PhD research project on sleep and source memory at The University of Texas. My boyfriend requested, more like pleaded and implored, that I join him.

"Oh, come on," he entreated. "It'll be fun. We even get to stay up all night together."

"To what end?" I asked. "I never pulled an all-nighter even for college finals."

"It's for research and it's important because it's for our age group: 65 to 75. Let's see how our memories hold up under sleep deprivation."

"Not good, I'm presuming," I said with doomsday reflection. "I really do dislike being put into an age category as if our brains are crumbling before our very eyes."

Our lovely and brilliant PhD candidate/researcher was persuasive and patient. She explained that we were volunteers in a particular method of research in which a problem is identified, relevant data are gathered, a hypothesis is formulated and then empirically tested.

Our experiment had two parts that tested memory and retention: In the first experiment, we had a 12-hour, stay-awake marathon ending at 6 a.m. with a pre- and post-series of memory tests. In the second experiment, we took a series of memory tests and then slept for 7 hours with electrodes plastered to our heads only to wake up and take another series of memory tests.

The purpose of the study was to investigate the behavioral responses to learning and memory tasks in 2 modes: sleep deprived and fully rested. Even though I took extensive surveys and questionnaires inquiring about my demographic, health, sleep, activities and cognitive abilities and tests that follow cognitive tasks that test attention, cognition, learning and some motor skills, I do not know my results.

I do know that it wasn't easy to watch my memory fail me again and again when I wasn't rested. When I had word recognition, I was thrilled because I knew my brain was working. With sleep deprivation, I was obviously not as sharp nor could I excel even if I wanted to. But when I had 7 hours of sleep, I was energized and did much better. I guess that was the point of all the staying awake.

My brain works pretty well in the moment, however, sometimes I lose the ability to reference past names, places and activities I once had at my fingertips. On the bright side, I just saw Graham Nash of Crosby, Stills & Nash and knew who he was instantly.

I focus on my *Challenge List for the Mind* to implement some reasonable practices to keep my mind strong:

Reduce resistance by eliminating defense mechanisms

Stay on the positive track by eliminating distractions

Eliminate negative self-talk and negative feelings

Learn to adapt and to accept change

Challenge your mind with new tasks & new ways of thinking

A closed mind is dangerous because it allows us to compartmentalize uncomfortable thoughts and feeling and that's a prescription for mindless repetition. Repetition can be a real brain killer.

The good news is there's no such thing as failure. You can stay up all night and beat the odds.

GPS OF THE MIND: KEEP DIRECTIONAL

Plutarch, Greek historian, biographer, and essayist wrote: "*The whole life of a man is but a point in time; let us enjoy it.*"

Plutarch's quote reminds me of a 4-year-old black Labrador dog called Nola, named for the city of New Orleans. After years of frustration, my son and daughter-in-law gave up trying to correct her obstreperous behavior. Her spirit would not be tamed. She was a totally loving, too exuberant a family dog who never meant harm when jumping on or barking at people entering the house.

Then one day Nola went blind. She developed a virus that quickly took her vision. We all cried, worried and wondered what would happen to her. At the moment Nola lost her vision, the whole of her life was but a point in time and she then continued to go forward enjoying every other point in time.

Nola has never stopped chasing balls, swimming, rolling on her back to be petted, gulping her food, sleeping at the foot of my son's bed or playing with her older sister and daily companion, a chocolate Labrador named Macy. From time to time, Nola loses her sense of direction, runs into walls and fails to find a thrown tennis ball, but her indomitable spirit trumps her handicap. Her GPS (Global Positioning System) is still directional, albeit with limitations.

Just as Nola lives with a GPS limitation so, too, do we humans. It might not be our eyesight, yet, from time to time, we can be sure there is something amiss in our GPS that gets us off track and prevents us from living an amazing and fulfilling life.

When Nola lost her sight, my son said, "Mom, you should write a blog about Nola and how amazing she is even without being able to see. She still has her GPS pretty much in tact." Of course, I said, "She still has her doggy determination."

Not only do we rely on our GPS in the car, but we also rely on the GPS of the mind. When reason or direction fails, we still have our moral, spiritual, emotional and physical compass. One chink in our human armor does not mean we cannot live with joy, inspiration and love.

Keep your GPS accurately directional by implementing some of these ideas:

Put the brain in a positive setting and celebrate life

Have you ever counted the number of times your mind goes to the negative during the day? I did that once – and only once because I was so surprised at the outcome. For every positive thought, I had at least three negative ones. I decided to train my brain to become more positive and change the formula for happiness with more gratitude and celebratory joy. My GPS is now firmly in a positive setting.

Change your reality lens

Sometimes your internal GPS does not perfectly reflect your reality lens. That's when we say, "Something is wrong with this picture." The duality of this internal/external reality is disconcerting. When you don't make a GPS correction, you find yourself in quicksand unable to move. Awareness coupled with mindful assessment can change the way we affect our reality.

Reduce stress by reducing resistance

Which comes first, the stress or the resistance? Or do they go together like a horse and carriage? If Nola failed to cope with her blindness, would she have exceeded herself? Of course, this was not the case. Nola knows no stress so her GPS is not affected by resistance. She leaps over obstacles and mental traps and confronts every point in time with energy and joy.

Buy experiences instead of things

The external world is not the predictor of happiness. It's the inner world, the GPS of the mind, that lets you experience everything with an open heart and mind. Things are material and transient. What stays constant and abiding is how your GPS allows you to experience the wonder and joys of life with clarity and passion.

Practice self-reflection every time you think about it

It is rare that you have time to reflect on your life. Self-reflection is considered a luxury these days instead of a necessity. Stress runs your life and you have no time to click on the GPS of the mind because instead of focusing and staying present, your mind is full of chatter, static and chaos. Set your GPS to enjoy every "point in time."

Remember, your GPS is you. And you are the only one who can measure your life, guide your life and ultimately fulfill your life in all its awesomeness just as Nola does every day.

....

THE BRINK
Well, I've been afraid of changing
'Cause I've built my life around you
But time makes you bolder
Even children get older
And I'm getting older too
- From Landslide by Fleetwood Mac

....

GET OUT OF THE WAY OF YOURSELF:
DON'T SELF-SABOTAGE

Getting in the way of ourselves, or, as some call this state – *being our own worst enemy* – has been around since the dawn of man. Modern psychology calls this syndrome *self-sabotaging behavior*. Sadly, self-sabotaging behavior seems to be ingrained in human nature.

According to *Psychology Today* (http://www.psychologytoday. com/basics/self-sabotage), self-sabotaging behavior comes in many forms "from procrastinating, to self-medication with one drug or another, to finding solace in comfort foods instead of exercise," or to a variety of unconscious self-injurious habits. Ongoing patterns of destructive behavior "undermine us, especially when we engage in them repeatedly."

On a broader spectrum, self-sabotage interferes with your values and your long-standing goals. Even if you realize that you are interfering with the best of who you are, there is no guarantee that you will stop self-sabotaging behavior. It's a constant temptation.

Every time you spend a moment getting in the way of personal growth, of personal satisfaction or discovery, is a moment of self-defeat. And you might not even know it because self-sabotaging behavior happens frequently in the smallest of ways. You might say, "I can't go on," "It's too difficult," "It can't be done," "I don't know how to do it," or "I give up." Where is my *white knight* to save me from disaster?" Are you really that helpless victim?

I spent last week under a kind of self-sabotaging frustration and it wasn't fun. For the life of me, I can't figure out oven clocks. Call me impaired and I am, but I tried to reset the stove clock after a power outage and for the life of me I couldn't do it. But I stayed with it for days and finally figured it out. That clock wasn't going to get the better of me. I'm no victim.

The same week my odometer decided to re-calibrate and lose about 8,000 miles. I read the owner's manual a dozen times to no avail. I couldn't move the odometer to the mileage that previously flashed on my dash. I spent days sitting in the car trying to recover those 8,000 miles. I finally took the car into the dealership. There was nothing wrong with my mileage. Problem solved. I'm not going to be anyone's victim.

In the two instances above, I solved my problems despite directions not being clear or even correct. I refused to be the victim of circumstances and refused to give up solving my problems. *I don't sabotage my problem-solving skills!*

I don't work in an office, but I can imagine that every day, several times a day, the self-sabotaging syndrome rears its ugly head. After spending hours and hours following directions for a specific program, you never achieve results. It just didn't work. You simply cannot actualize a positive outcome. You complain and you insist the directions were wrong. Are you the victim?

Wouldn't it be awesome if there were some sort of turn-off valve, some barrier that would protect you from needless emotional struggles and set you on a path of actualizing your full human potential?

According to the online magazine, *PsychAlive, Psychology for Everyday:*

Knowing where self-sabotaging thoughts come from can be the first step in controlling your self-defeating behaviors.

Everyone hides myriad childhood influences and experiences that make you *your own worst enemy.* There are behavioral therapies aimed at interrupting ingrained self-sabotaging patterns. These therapies stop thought, that is interrupt it, letting the thought go or redirecting it into positive statements.

But no one can teach you *not* to give up but *YOU.*

Since everyone is a talented individual with natural gifts given at birth, you can teach yourself to resist self-sabotaging behavior in favor of channeling and strengthening your talents and abilities toward solving problems with commitment and, therefore, build happier and more positive mindsets.

Focus on the following mutually supportive 3 R S to finally, once and for all, eliminate the self-sabotaging syndrome:

Resourcefulness
Resourcefulness implies the ability to move through difficult situations. It does not imply that there will be a successful outcome or that you'll have the ability to solve a problem with ease.

The skill of being resourceful encompasses the ability to access your imagination, your inventiveness, and the aptitude to think *beyond* the situation that involves the difficulty.

Resilience
Psychology Today defines resilience as that "ineffable quality that allows some people to be knocked down by life and come back stronger than ever. Rather than letting failure overcome you and drain your resolve, you find a way to rise from the ashes." Resilience implies adaptation to adversity. It also implies the ability to endure past the point of simply "just giving up in the face of difficulty."

Resoluteness
There is an element of tenacity, steadfastness and competence in problem solving. Resoluteness implies a strong tolerance for finding solutions even in the face of adverse responses. Resoluteness has paved the way for tremendous progress in science and technology for centuries.

Finding solutions to solving challenging problems or forging through life's adversities can be a rewarding and positive experience. Implementing the 3RS – resourcefulness, resilience and resoluteness – can be a helpful checkpoint in eliminating self-sabotaging behavior. The 3RS will also provide increased focus on your most important goals and values.

It's an epidemic – not like the Ebola virus, Nile virus, Dengue fever, polio, SARS or even Legionnaires disease. The epidemic I'm referring to is the *need to be right!*

Almost everyone living on this planet feels the need to be right. The *need to be right* is the most important way the ego is satisfied. It doesn't matter if other people are hurt, maimed or killed in the act of your need *to be right*. The need-to-be-right syndrome feels good and no one is going to take that away from you. Long live your ego!

If I were inclined to feel a little generous toward the human race after years of being exposed to wars and the global killing fields, I might give mankind a break and proffer that all this cruel and brutal behavior is a result of the worst inclinations of man's collective unconscious. Yet, these despicable atrocities seem to have some esoteric purpose, and frankly I'm not in the mood to cut mankind a break.

Humankind knows no limits when it comes to *needing to be right*. Nobody's opinion or idea has any value or worth outside of *your agenda*. It's an absurd premise and here's why:

People who have to be right find themselves alone and isolated from groups of friends, colleagues or families. They hold on to their righteous ideology and opinions so tightly that no one can have a reasonable dialogue with them.

The need to be right becomes a crusade. Even though they might suffer emotionally, physically and intellectually, they never notice the negative effects or debilitating psychic downward spiral. Pushing their ideological agenda, these people fail to realize that they are more than the thought they are projecting.

The need to be right does not respect the individuality of others. Every person is born with unique DNA. Every brain is wired differently. What you think comes from your nurture and nature just as what I think comes from different constructs. This suggests a need for mutual respect.

If someone can't let go of *having to be right*, their mindset becomes rigid and fixed in patterns that prevent openness to others, to new ideas and opportunities. For them, life stands still. Worse, they are stuck in the past. There is no future.

The need to be right destroys the possibility of entertaining alternatives. Webster's dictionary defines the word *right* as "conforming to facts or truth; most favorable or desired." This definition melds truth with fact. Whose truth? Whose fact? What if two different viewpoints each conform to the truth? Which is more right? Is one person's truth another person's fiction?

The need to be right leads to self-destructive behavior. It's human nature to perceive people who *have to be right* as know-it-alls. This implacable attitude conjures up self-righteousness and pictures of people who are alienated from interaction in society. The general perception is they are not team players and don't work well with others. They are hard to get along with. They turn away connectedness and love.

The need to be right kills curiosity. People who *have to be right* do not practice active listening. They don't hear what's going on in the environment. If they don't listen, they never learn anything new. Curiosity dies slowly and in the end nothing but validation will ever interest a person who has to be right. For a mind to develop, it needs to entertain alternative thoughts, ideas and desires. How do you learn if not through others?

The need to be right is not worth the struggle. It takes so much energy for people to *have to be right.* Sometimes it even takes weapons and brutality to keep their ideas alive and spreading to others. Those who take ideas to extremes with a single-minded purpose and never notice different shades of gray are the true losers in their fight to keep their beliefs alive.

If people didn't *need to be* right, they might notice things differently and start to accept change as not only inevitable, but also good. They might recognize they are feeling happier because they are more connected. They might accept new possibilities for a more meaningful and fulfilling life.

KEEP UP WITH YOUR LIFE, DUDE

I was sitting with a new friend at a popular local coffee shop in Austin talking about the truths of life when my friend threw me a curve ball, "Are you keeping up with your life now that you're brand new to Austin?"

Hold on a second! How did we get from *moving beyond religion to me keeping up with my life*?

The idea that I had to think about keeping up with my life never occurred to me. Was it possible that I was leaving my life behind me every day I lived more of it? No, that was too *existential* an idea considering we were talking about more spiritual matters – more along the lines of subjective experience and psychological growth outside the bounds of a religious context.

Maybe my friend was referring in a general sense to any kind of meaningful activity or blissful experience and was asking if I was consciously mindful of the creative process called life.

How much are you a part of your life – 50%, 70%, 100%? And how much are you responsible for your wholeness as a human being? Are you keeping up with your life and not the lives of others? How good are you at keeping up with the nitty-gritty of life instead of buying into the distractions that take us away from our core beliefs and values?

The following are a few ways to successfully keep up with your life:

Recognize that you are consciousness
Your thoughts have a rippling effect throughout your body. Therefore, what you think consciously creates who you are. Focus on abundance of health, love and prosperity, and that is what you will receive. Be open to thoughts of kindness and that is what you will receive. By acknowledging that your mindset has the ability to change, you will successfully keep up with your life.

Find peace within the chaotic sequence of life
The last two weeks my Austin family has experienced one chaotic moment after another, culminating in their beloved dog being put down. My daughter-in-law and I talked about turning the chaos around and finding peace within daily happenstance. In every chaotic moment, the intuitive instinct for peace presents an opportunity to connect the mind, body and spirit into an integrated and well-balanced person. That's when you successfully keep up with your life.

Get mastery over self
When I began my yoga practice more than 20 years ago, I heard a mantra from my teachers about the importance of gaining self-mastery. Over the course of my yoga practice, I began to understand that self-mastery asks you to gain control over your mind and emotions by eliminating fears based on limiting beliefs and distractions that constantly get in the way of staying 100% present in your environment. Self-mastery is not only a path to successfully keeping up with your life, but is also the path to happiness.

Give gratitude daily
Gratitude is an awareness that what makes your life creative and loving will inspire you to give more of yourself. Gratitude

says: *I am sufficient unto the needs of myself.* Gratitude builds your dreams and establishes the foundation in life and work. Give gratitude for your gifts, talents and blessings many times throughout the day and you will successfully keep up with your life.

Be kind to yourself
Before others can be kind to you, you must be kind to yourself. Kindness to self reflects your core beliefs and these values identify your life's path. The ability to be kind to yourself comes from the practice of self-reflection. If you are secure in your authentic self and if you embrace the abundance you possess, you will not only give the gift of kindness to yourself, but you will extend your kindness to others in your environment. Then everyone will successfully keep up with life!

If you are truly connected to your life in all manner of your existence, you will successfully keep up with your life. Living is a creative expression of what makes you who you are. Think of the joy when everyone sits at the table of life without fear of being judged or labeled, living freely, dancing freely and giving freely.

TO RISK OR NOT TO RISK: THAT IS THE QUESTION

Every so often a situation arises that feels like it might shake the very foundation of your being or at least considerably discombobulate your comfort zone.

When this happens, your inclination can be to bury the negative feelings under the rug and keep those mind/body/spirit rumblings locked in a box deep in the unconscious zone. Who wants to be challenged by the unknown? Recognizing your own vulnerability has a way of complicating life.

It happened to me two years ago when my comfort zone was thrown off balance by the nagging feeling that it was time to leave Los Angeles and move to Austin.

Unconsciously, I knew it was the correct move, yet consciously I realized I would be taking a huge leap of faith. Leaving LA after 30 years was psychologically and emotionally risky. I'm a California girl from birth, and I identify politically and culturally with all that symbolizes its lifestyle. LA and I have major history.

My conundrum about leaving LA was persistent. Doubts about living in a sprawling city in my 70s posed real concerns. I needed friendlier city energy and an easier lifestyle. I was restless and feeling confined by daily traffic issues and parking challenges.

I missed being close to my family, especially my grandchildren. I was flying monthly from LA to Las Vegas then to Austin. I endured years of 405 freeway closures, road work on major streets, spending more time driving the two miles to UCLA than teaching my yoga and meditation classes.

I began to make choices to go or not to go tango dancing based on the length of the drive to Hollywood or the Valley. Car culture was clawing at my soul even though I learned to meditate in my Jetta while stuck on a freeway. Was this really the life I wanted to live?

Recently, I saw *The Theory of Everything*, a movie about the life and work of Stephen Hawking. I was emotionally moved by his extraordinary feat of living life in a body that had shut down while possessing a mind that functioned at the highest level of intelligence. I began to muse on the real meaning of being brave.

Being brave is different for everyone. For some, bravery means taking a risk in the face of difficulty or adversity and overcoming fear. It's easier to read about brave heroes and warriors in history who take risks and follow a strong moral compass than it is to actually be brave in reality. When you think of Lincoln freeing the slaves, European explorers discovering new worlds, scientists discovering new theories about our universe, martyrs and heroes who died for a higher truth, we intuitively know that these are the risk takers who define bravery.

I'm simply an ordinary mortal faced with the question "to risk or not to risk" in a micro setting. And even though I'm not one of history's brave souls, all humans have one condition in common, a heart that speaks to us and takes us on the true path of our journey. The yogi's mantra *live your truth* is ever present in my soul.

In September, I was about to leave my position as a yoga and meditation teacher at UCLA without having assessed the risk – making that clear decision to move to Austin – when, riding in the elevator one day in the Engineering and Math Building I encountered one of my students. After a few moments of silence, she suddenly asked:

"How did you know that you had to leave teaching and move to another city?"

Then she added, "I think that is really amazing that you came to that conclusion. All your students are impressed and supportive."

Faced with the reality of somebody else pondering the potential of taking a risk, I stumbled on an answer, "My heart says I need different experiences to keep my life interesting and creative."

In one of the speeches I give as a keynote speaker, I challenge my audience to take risks, plenty of leaps of faith and be willing to make glorious mistakes. It always occurs to me as I speak that I'm actually challenging myself.

I know that playing it safe offers little contrast in life. The joys are in the surprises, in the details and delights of every-day life, in thumbing your nose at the status quo, driving your grandchildren to school in the chill, crisp air of an Austin winter morning and dancing the two step at the Broken Spoke down the street from my new apartment in the hippest part of Austin.

To risk or not to risk is not the most important question anymore because I realize that 71 is a great age to make a change and experience the slings and arrows of outrageous fortune and to take arms against inertia. The odds are better than you think that you'll come across amazing possibilities and opportunities because in my heart I know there is no such thing as failure. There is only personal truth and professional integrity and they are always there for the taking anywhere you choose to live.

Besides, Austin was just ranked 7th as one of the best cities for successful aging.

BOTH SIDES NOW
I've looked at clouds from both sides now
From up and down and still somehow
It's cloud illusions I recall
I really don't know clouds at all
- From *Both Sides Now,* lyrics and music by Judy Collins

INVISIBLE FORCES SHAPE YOUR LIFE: THE GURU ABIDES

Is the life you worked so hard to create actually what you thought it was going to be? You've achieved success, but are you happy? Fulfilled? Do material things shape your life or does your inner guru – the invisible force inside yourself – shape what matters to you?

William James, long considered the father of modern psychology, wrote: "*The greatest discovery of my generation is that a human being can alter his life by altering his attitudes...Each of us literally chooses, by his way of attending to things, what sort of universe he shall appear to himself to inhabit.*"

Your life, your universe, emanates from an image held with faith and focus on all the invisible elements of your world – including everything you have ever done, ever been, or ever thought about in your world. That image then attracts whatever it is you want, desire or need.

In essence, you are your own guru, your own teacher and master of the invisible forces that shape your life.

However, if your mantra is *he who has the gold, wins*, you are living in a fog of limiting beliefs. Your material possessions don't represent who you really are, they don't fulfill your potential, create permanent happiness or help you find true and honest relationships.

When you become fully conscious of the power of your inner guru and discover the forces that shape your life, your choices and decisions will lead you to a fulfilling and peaceful life.

We all possess invisible forces and here are a few of my favorites:

Resourcefulness: The Defining Force
Sometimes life throws you curve balls and you meet the unexpected. How do you get back on track and deal with things as they are and not as you want them to be?

The defining force in life is the ability to be resourceful with intention and focus. Intention creates clarity of thought. Focus is a matter of listening to your inner voice as to how to carry out the intention. Resourcefulness allows you to exceed your aspirations and removes stumbling blocks to living an enriched life.

One of my yoga students called me the other day to ask how I'm doing after my cross-country move. "I'm great," I said.

"If you landed in the middle of the African continent, you'd be fine," he remarked.

Would you have the inner resources to create an alternative path if the one you are presently on isn't fulfilling or isn't making you happy?

An Open Mind

How many times in your life have people tried to judge you and mess with your head and heart? How quickly did it take you to realize that someone else was entering your personal space? And what did you do about it?

Keeping an open mind without others' influence is the first step to unleashing the unlimited power within you. You've been given the power to develop ideas and exercise free will. With a keen sense of who you are, you can take self-judgment and the judgment of others out of the decision-making process.

Emotional Fitness

How often do you wake up every morning thinking about the past – the mistakes made, the regrets, carry-forward anger, self-abuse and a litany of other feelings long gone?

Emotional fitness means clearing the mind of negative thoughts so you can cut through the clutter and achieve balance. On my off-balance days, I have too much negative backlash in body, mind and spirit. That tells me it's time to dial down the stress, revive my energy and get back to my guru self and master what matters to me most in life.

Connection

The other gurus, the big dudes who understand the mysteries of life, know that connection to others means love. And love means a generosity of spirit that constantly reminds us that we are living abundant lives.

Connection removes the scarcity mentality. It is the prerequisite to happiness. The values of connection fill the pages of health articles everywhere, a stronger immune system, longevity, an enriched life, and plenty of self-esteem. If you listen closely, your inner guru will encourage you to love and connect everything on the planet with a sense of continuity that will enhance the quality of your life.

Certainty vs. Uncertainty: The Flip Side of the Coin
Life is full of surprises. No one is lumbering under the illusion that there is certainty in life, yet, uncertainty abounds.

A mental state of prolonged uncertainty affects you negatively. It causes stress, anxiety and fear. As a result, decisions take longer to make, and while you are deciding a course of action, you become compromised or stuck. This kind of paralysis prevents you from moving your life forward with clarity or conviction. Uncertainty is also influenced by the expectations imposed by society and the mindless mental distractions that keep you in a state of confusion and denial. When you lose your *inner, all-knowing voice,* you are giving up gaining control over your life.

Take time every day to listen without distraction to your guru in meditation and create room for your inner voice to speak to you.

There are indeed invisible forces that shape your life, however, if you have an appreciation of and value for the invisible forces within yourself, you will be reminded of who you are and what you can accomplish.

Your guru does not judge, your guru does not fear, your guru abides.

Do you ever wonder why some people are successful and accomplished in business, but not very successful in their personal lives?

This question came up when I was dating a famous musician who had a successful music career not only as a guitarist, but also as a music producer and composer, yet for years he couldn't create a personal life that reflected the success of his professional life.

I eventually let the relationship go, but I still wondered why some very successful and accomplished men and women in business and the arts have personal lives that don't measure up to their obvious talents.

One of my friends ran a highly successful Internet sales company. When he took his company public, investment money came into his business and profits soared. Yet this man's personal life was in shambles – a marriage long ago broken, incredible daily stress, and poor interpersonal relationships with friends and family. He didn't apply the skills of his professional success to his personal life.

If you take the skills required to be a top talent in business and apply them to creating a successful personal life, the dichotomy between your professional and personal life will be minimized.

Following our breakup, I compiled a list of a few of my favorite professional skills that can make one's personal life more successful:

Adapt quickly
Because top, talented people are extremely quick learners, they are willing to move in new directions when analyzing a problem that needs to be solved. Talented people keep an open mind, deal with unexpected situations quickly, integrate and prioritize new information all while remaining calm and composed under stress.

Willing to collaborate
Working or living with others is usually a collaborative experience. People who collaborate identify the best person to do the job and what will work effectively with the team dynamic. They have clear communication skills, get along well with others and don't fear negative feedback.

Embrace problem solving
A problem solver is usually a creative person who inspires and leads others to participate in overcoming obstacles to success. Their intuitive skill set allows them to see real or potential problems quickly helping the team to overcome issues and problems.

Create good habits
Many high-achieving professionals claim their success is due to routines that manage their time and ensure productivity. As a result, fewer mistakes are made.

Constructive habits help achieve daily as well as strategic goals. Being consistent in habits is crucial for creating clear boundaries with order and consistency.

Work toward being more balanced
Balance is built on knowledge of how every part of the business integrates into a structure that runs efficiently with cost containment. Balance keeps the professional self-directed, motivated as well as more mindful and creative.

Demonstrate accountability
Accountability demonstrates attributes of honesty and responsibility. To be accountable, the successful professional creates structure, develops a consistent routine and takes incremental steps to achieve goals.

Humble thyself
The humble professional exhibits a level of confidence without intimidation. Confidence comes from full knowledge of the company structure. The humble approach calmly fosters a sense of openness as employees face daily challenges.

In my experience, practicing just some of these professional skills consistently in your personal life will give you reliable and successful outcomes. Clear actions result in less confusion, doubt and uncertainty in life. More importantly, the people closest to you will have the reassurance of your support and love – and that's what success is all about.

· ·

UP ON THE ROOF
When this old world starts a getting me down,
and people are just too much for me to face.
I'll climb way up to the top of the stairs and all my cares just drift right into space.
On the roof, it's peaceful as can be and there the world below don't bother me, no, no.
- from Up On The Roof, Lyrics by James Taylor

· ·

DON'T FREAK OUT: FREE YOUR MIND AND FIND SUCCESS

My best friend's son had a rough go of it for the last several years. A vulture capitalist engineered a takeover and he lost his company of 11 years. For the last year and a half, he was a CFO of a company that owned properties and franchises. He was unhappy about its lackluster attempts to expand and reach its full potential.

For several years, my friend's son has been consulting with a therapist who specializes in setting professional goals. She guides a client toward *freeing up the mind space* and developing greater perspective in regard to achieving optimal happiness. The end result is a healthy detachment and freedom from prioritizing the company over achieving personal success.

Freeing Up Space In Your Mind

The concept of freeing up space in your mind might seem uncomfortable at first because it takes you outside your comfort zone. To some, free mind space represents confusion, doubt and fear. To others, free mind space represents possibilities and opportunities – *the world is your oyster.*

The therapist suggested that no mind could be free in a state of anger and disappointment. Once free of the negativity that occupies more space in your mind than you realize, you will be able to consciously free up your thoughts and desires.

Space can set free the unlimited power within you for personal and professional growth. Space will also give you focused awareness about what the unconscious mind is identifying as important.

Here are some suggestions that will free up mind space and alter the trajectory of your life's journey:

Down Time Is Up Time
When I'm not working, there is a reason for it. I call it fallow time, time to regroup and get in touch with my feelings. I think of the farmers who planted crops for several years in one field and then let that field go fallow while nature replenished the soil. Down time is for personal growth. What might add to the happiness quotient to your work and life?

Stop Being the Judger

People who judge other people assume they have knowledge of another's circumstance. In my family, any member, child or adult, who thinks they are the boss of someone else is called *the* judger. We make fun of anyone who gets caught making judgments by loudly proclaiming, *Here come the judgers.* We remind the judger to *get over yourself because you don't know anything about what's going on!*

Over a lifetime you collect ideas from parents, society, friends, history, teachers, ministers, the media and the Internet. The world is full of opinions, and they are just that – opinions. And opinions create judgments. However, other people's beliefs are not yours. Judging closes down the mind. Instead of labeling, free your mind to decide what adds value to your life, what makes *you* happy and what code of ethics you must follow to live a fulfilling life. Please don't live in another person's head.

Learn to Meditate

One of the best ways to create space in your mind, to think freely and with conscious awareness, is to clear the mind and come into a relaxed physical and mental state. This is called *meditation.* The results are amazing: You clear out the mind clutter, dial down stress, manage overwhelming feelings and energize your environment. Personal empowerment is the result.

Master What Matters To You

You change, you grow, and you often transform yourself from one thing to another. I was focused and passionate about each stage of my life and I was happily and fully involved and committed. Master what matters to you and that one thing will deliver extraordinary results in every area of your life.

When you free the mind, you overcome distractions that get in the way of what matters most to you personally and professionally. Creating open space in your mind will increase your focus and confidence and enhance the quality of your life.

YOU'RE A GENIUS AND YOU DIDN'T EVEN KNOW IT

I'm reading Walter Isaacson's latest book, *The Innovator,* a historical retelling of how math and science innovators throughout the centuries, beginning in the 1700s to the present, conceived and attempted to execute technological advances that lead to what we know today as the Internet universe. It took me three weeks to get past page 20.

Reading the early chapters of how a few selected genius thinkers – energized first by a female scientist in the 1700s – created a mindset that attempted to aggregate information for an outcome not immediately apparent to me. I spent night after night plowing through two or three pages trying to understand the math and science of it all.

Finally, it occurred to me that analog or digital formats, vacuum tubes and tin cans all added up to creating systems and machines that would eventually manage and code information.

These geniuses were imagining today's world! Their innovations would eventually become stunning, world-altering innovations, especially in the technological arena in the late 19th and 20th centuries. The Internet was being planned well before it became a reality.

Creativity takes novel or even off-the-wall ideas and re-envisions them in useful and appealing ways. The end result is something new and fresh, fascinating and revealing. Genius happens when creativity moves away from *expectation*.

In other words, creativity occurs when an individual visualizes a new way or a new pattern that generates an idea or several ideas that don't fit into the norms of cultural expectations. It is the ability of the creative mind to recognize patterns that create the basis for a new product or service that makes our life exciting and inspiring. Think: Edison and the light bulb; Steve Jobs and the personal computer; Thomas Crapper and the flushing toilet.

And then, of course, it is the role of the innovative, the outcome of creativity to challenge existing norms, to produce more radical ideas and communicate these patterns to others. If you read Walter Isaacson's book on Steve Jobs, you begin to understand how an extreme creative process innovated our technical world and turned it upside down.

The ability to see the connections between things that you previously thought were not connectable is a valuable and wise commodity not only in business, but also in life. Creativity produces different viewpoints that require broad knowledge and a fair amount of collaboration. The result is that creativity changes lives.

Stimulating creativity and finding your inner genius is not for the faint of heart.

Creativity Takes Courage

Taking risks is not inherently part of human nature because stepping outside your comfort zone poses a challenge. You fear failure, criticism or indifference. It's fairly obvious that creativity and fear don't go together, but taking a few risks, making some mistakes and plenty of leaps of faith makes life productive and fulfilling.

No Limits On Journey

Limitations that are in the mind of the beholder have no place in the creativity zone. Rigid perceptions and uncompromising expectations, past experiences or a preoccupation with outcomes rather than process are barriers to creativity. But the most significant barrier is uncertainty. There are no guarantees, so why not take time everyday to create space in your brain and ask, *"what more can I contribute to my job or how can I make my life more passionate and exciting?"*

Don't Get Separated From the Source of Your Thinking

If you dare to think differently, or if you dare to think beyond the obvious, or below the surface, or beyond cause and effect, you are thinking creatively. Some people call that *thinking like a freak*. If you are *told* what to do, you get separated from the source of your thinking. You are the source of creativity, not the external commands or the go-to cause and effect. Freaky is fun.

Be Vulnerable

Starting from the point of awareness of your own vulnerability, from your palate of senses, feelings, intuition, you can dare greatly. Gay Gaddis, the owner and founder of T3 (*The Think Tank*), a top integrated marketing firm that specializes in innovative marketing campaigns, said: *"When you shut down vulnerability, you shut down opportunity."* There is no vision without vulnerability.

You Are Already A Genius

The Dalai Lama said: *"When you talk, you are already repeating what you know. But if you listen, you may learn something new."*

Listening generates new ideas and encourages taking new paths. Listening gives you the opportunity to distinguish yourself. Your music might be another's noise or your disaster might be another person's photo op, but pay no attention. What you have is unique – you have genius.

THE BUCKET LIST: 5 TOOLS FOR SETTING AND FOCUSING ON GOALS

I was a participant at the Healthy Aging Conference – *Taking Control of Your Life* hosted by the UCLA Longevity Center Fall Conference 2012. Since I am definitely a boomer and senior, Dr. Gary Small, Director of the UCLA Longevity Center at the Semel Institute for Neuroscience and Human Behavior, thought I'd be a good fit to serve on a panel titled *The Bucket List: Setting and Focusing On Goals.* Needless to say, I was excited about speaking on a subject that would be important to boomers and seniors as they continue to develop a healthy mental and physical lifestyle.

Identifying tools for creating and executing a plan for lifelong vitality and setting up a personal Bucket List are fascinating and sometimes perplexing.

After all, life doesn't come to you; you create the life you want and deserve. And I'm pretty sure every human on this planet wants to live life to the fullest.

As a motivational speaker and yoga and meditation instructor at UCLA, I'm 24/7 concerned about maximizing our human potential. After all, isn't that what our lives are all about? When I speak to audiences, I like to shake up the myths about growing older and turn those perceptions upside down. This requires a different mindset about the exciting opportunities ahead of you as the decades pass by.

The concept inherent in the bucket list is that life is not always about *what happens to you,* but about *what you do with what happens to you.* It's about making choices that claim the highest level of your well being and that includes having the ability to realize your dreams and passions no matter your age.

Let's face it, we're living longer and the idea that boomers or seniors are going to sit around participating in some ancient retirement ritual is simply not applicable or relevant in the 21st century. There is a new sense of freedom knocking at our door.

I suggested to the audience five simple, effective tools to ascertain and prepare for selecting that all-important bucket list. I was sure everyone in the audience had entertained these five tools at some point, but perhaps they haven't thought of using them in the context of what was most important to them.

If we spend some time getting to know ourselves, our capabilities and desires, the choices we make to fill our bucket list will be the right choices for us. Remember not to limit your thinking.

These 5 tools are lifelong challenges for conscious living:

Have a daily *attitude of gratitude* and create inspiration and positive energy for living.

Be vulnerable and recognize vulnerability as a way to create and innovate.

Learn to adapt and seize the opportunities for growth and change.

Find your passion and never limit yourself by conforming to someone else's idea of who you are.

Practice forgiveness as a way of releasing negativity in your life.

So take the plunge and make a list that is perfectly outrageous and meet me at the top of Kilimanjaro where I'll be doing a headstand.

PART 3
Stay Strong

Let's look at your life as a giant goodie basket. This basket contains everything you are as an individual. You are a gold mine of thoughts, emotions, passions, dreams, and virtues. Everything that has happened to you – your losses, successes, struggles, joys, fulfillments and everything you have experienced goes into this goodie basket and teaches you how to take charge of your life.

Of course, your life hasn't always come up roses. You've faced some difficulties and more than your fair share of struggles. Yet, how can you appreciate and have gratitude for the abundance in life if you never see contrasts or feel what it's like to change your negative mindsets?

You will always get stronger and smarter by embracing all aspects of your life. That's life. Welcome it!

What's truly exciting about life is that you are always in process. You are not rehearsing for another life. This is it! It's the only one you know about.

I'm going to offer you a challenge: I want you to create the most AWESOME life imaginable – fulfilling, joyful, productive, creative, sprinkled with courage to take some risks, make glorious mistakes, and plenty leaps of faith.

There are no limits on this journey. Any limitations are a result of your own perceptions and expectations, past experiences or pre-occupations with outcomes and goals rather than process – all of which can set you up for self-induced dependence.

Maybe you've wanted to be the boss of you for a long time and haven't. What's holding you back: money, health, a relationship, a job? These are some of the limitations you might experience and they are called excuses, excuses not to be the boss of you, not to take charge of your life fully and richly.

Excuses are inherently not character enhancing. Some might call them character defects – like blaming others or projecting your sense of failure onto others. No matter what limitation or excuse is holding you back from maximizing your human potential, there is something deeper inside of you adding to your confusion – and it's called *resistance.*

Resistance is a psychological defensive mechanism that causes you to reject, deny or otherwise oppose action. Whether it's the life we live on the outside or our inside life – our passions and dreams – it's human nature to resist.

Stephen Pressfield, in his book *The War of Art* calls resistance "the most toxic force on the planet; the root of more unhappiness than poverty, disease, and erectile dysfunction; it crushes our spirit and makes us less than we were born to be."

That's really boring because resistance allows us to make endless excuses not to do what we really want to do. I'm too busy, I'm too old, I'm too young, I'm too fat, I need a nap, I'll do it tomorrow, I'm not good enough or competent enough. Sound familiar? Resistance depletes your resourcefulness and your ability to make good decisions that move your life forward with strength.

You are the only one that can defeat resistance. Every morning, every day, one day at a time, get up with an intention to do the most important thing in your life – something that brings you joy and satisfaction, gives you positive energy, fulfills a need and lights your fire! Every day be vigilant, be aware, and be clear about what you want to do so you can bring balance and focus into your life.

When I first started my speaking journey, I was convinced that my signature keynote speech was going to be *Retirement Is Not an Option* for Baby Boomers. Boomers still had Act 3 ahead of them and I decided I would enlighten them as to how to make the most of it.

I soon realized that was a limiting idea. My message wasn't just for Boomers headed toward retirement; it was much more than that. I was fortunate to find a brilliant brander to help me broaden my message. Yet, for more than a month, I resisted her advice. I couldn't or wouldn't wrap my head around what she was asking me to do: think bigger about who I am and more deeply about how my message and themes could have a larger scope and resonate more profoundly.

Finally, out of exasperation, I said to her: "Okay, okay, I'm resisting you and your message! I don't want to do what you ask – to think more about who I am and what I need to say."

Just as I said it, I had a vision – one of those Saul on the Road to Damascus conversions and I knew I could and would create a larger context for speaking. I began to see possibilities and opportunities because I stopped resisting and moved into speaking about, ironically enough, "stretching the mind at any age," making great decisions and bringing work and life into balance.

If the Road to Damascus revelation hasn't yet happened for you, I encourage you to practice meditation to clear your mind. Meditation creates a positive open mind, one that is disciplined rather than distracted. Meditation frees up mind space so you can define your needs while linking up significant emotional and spiritual connections.

With the clarity of thought that meditation provides, I've been able to break several habits in my life that didn't contribute to my health or happiness. Some of these habits depleted my ability to remain strong and took away my energy to sustain my mind, body and spirit connection. Too many times I let my emotional needs and connections to men get in the way of my life's path.

I remember when I finally snapped out being emotionally obsessed with boyfriends that no longer added to my happiness and often made me a victim of myself. I saw the 2004 part documentary/part fiction, *What The Bleep Do We Know?*

It is the story about a young girl thrown into crisis as she questions the fundamental premise of her life – that what she has believed about men, how relationships should be, and how her emotions affect her work aren't reality at all. The protagonist begins to relax into an experience that allows her to see reality as it is and not as her imagination wants it to be. She conquers her fears and gains wisdom because she is no longer a victim of circumstances. She is on her way to being a creative force in her life and her life will never be the same.

It's challenging to break habits that don't add value to your life. I've noticed that if my mind is cluttered and unclear and if my environment is messy and filled with unnecessary things, I don't think clearly.

More than 40 years ago when I was separating from my husband, I had to clear out the contents of a very large home. I discovered it was relativity easy for me to let go of material things. I never knew that about myself until I had to pack up my house. I knew there was something good about my divorce because it was the beginning of my commitment to live light and to eliminate things that I no longer needed. Later, through meditation, I learned that material things are transitory, and I'm now living only with what is absolutely essential for me.

When I left Los Angeles for Austin, I let go of everything except the most important books, art and memories from my parents and children. Eliminating the unnecessary clears space for what adds value to my well being.

Maybe you'll break a habit, eliminate something superfluous in your life, or do something that makes you feel insecure, strange or frightened. Maybe you'll carry out an action with complete attention and intensity as if it were your last and start today to live a life that reflects your values, your needs and desires. Even Lululemon asks you do one thing a day that scares you. I do a headstand every day to remind myself to be brave.

Staying strong begins with the idea of maximizing your human potential in all aspects of your life. If you can see your life as a circle with equal parts living harmoniously within you, everything is possible. There will be no struggle. There will be no stress. You'll have the freedom to seize the moment, eliminate those who distract you and get in the way of your happiness, and reflect daily on your intentions.

Get ready! Get set! And live a life that will be balanced, richly nuanced and full to capacity. And that smile will never leave your beautiful face.

IF NOT NOW, WHEN?

You've all heard the phrase so many times it has become a universal mantra:

If not now, when?

I repeated that same mantra to myself in March, 1984. I was standing backstage at the Old Globe Theater in San Diego and waiting for my cue. The woman in front of me was no other than Marion Ross, the quintessential mother in the hit TV series, *Happy Days*. Marion was in the same drab, unexciting play written by a Hungarian about, what else, but Hungarians! I was playing the younger daughter of the master of the house. My character added absolutely nothing to the story – whatever the story may have been because I truly can't remember.

I was shifting from one leg to another in a rather unhappy state when I blurted out to anyone that might be listening (sotto voce, of course) that I was sick of waiting for my cue to go onstage and pretend to be someone else. I wanted to live a real life – my own life! Marion turned around and looked at me.

"Why, darling," she said, "Do you need my permission because I'll give it to you if you want."

"Yes," I said sheepishly, "I guess I do."

Then Marian Said to me: "If not now, when. Go! You have the power to do whatever you want to do in life and you don't need my permission. I've never asked permission for anything in my life, even when people told me not to go on something called television back in the 1950s in a show called, *Life With Father*. They thought I would tank my career. And look at me now! Some tank!"

And with that she turned around, heard her cue, and walked elegantly on stage. I followed closely behind and felt the backdraft of her royal presence not as an actress, but as a woman and as a human being who was in full control of her life. She was fearless.

I left the theater after that dreadful play closed and never looked back. I began the next phase of my glorious journey. I learned two things from Marion Ross:

We don't need permission to do anything in life – get married, get divorced, travel around the world, weave carpets – because we can darn well make our own personal choices; and,

Don't wait to do the things you want to do – if not now, when? It is only then that we are walking our own path. It is only then that we know who we are.

If not now, when? If I'm not for myself, who will be? If I'm not making the brave, strong choices that make a difference in my life, then I am definitely sinking in quicksand. But if life is good and you are in it for the long run, then you have to make something out of it. You have to be willing to sweat for it; you have to commit to something!

Life is a privilege. Life is a gift. Life is good and we're waist deep in it.

Humans are all about creating energy. Our thoughts are energy and that energy turns to matter and the matter turns back in to us. It is imperative that we manage our thoughts, clear out our mental environment and stay true to ourselves.

We are the authors of our own story, and we have to seriously consider not being so quick to give our story to someone else or design our story by the trend of any group or the zeitgeist of our culture.

It is a challenge to stay on our path because along the way we emotionally associate with the habits and reactions of outside stimuli: parents, teachers, friends, coworkers, and celebrities. In time, we come to believe these behaviors and values are, in fact, our own beliefs. Over and over we continually reinforce our learned group behavior and beliefs and in so doing lose our own inner voice.

Yet, we can reclaim our own positive sense of self by making small intentions. Intentions come from the practice of being fully conscious of our needs and desires. That's how we move forward in life.

Joseph Campbell writes in his book, *Pathways to Bliss*, that to live healthy, age well and bring your life into balance, it is necessary to create small intentions within your immediate and natural environment to be true to yourself.

Marion Ross was already clued into Joseph Campbell and was true to herself. I learned from her to follow my heart and make intentions about what makes me happy and that translates into a reality filled with simple, elegant, and positive experiences.

If not now, when?

THE WONDER YEARS

I started my period at 13 and my mother gave me a pamphlet about menstruating instead of talking to me about it. I was bursting out of my size A bra and began to notice that I was growing major, significant breasts. Underarm hair was also a new phenomenon. When I entered high school, my breasts grew from an A to a D in about 10 seconds and I suddenly became very popular at Marin Catholic High School.

Don't get me wrong; I was popular at St. Raphael's grammar school too, even without the boobs. I wasn't a great beauty, but I was the class clown and that gave me, as they say today, *street cred*. I knew I had to make my mark in social circles because I had a chipped front tooth. The class clown label distracted from its ugliness. Finally in 6th grade I got a cap on my tooth and was able to get a boyfriend and neck (old fashioned for make out) with Ronnie Denman in the back row of the Raphael Movie Theater. Being funny wasn't so important anymore. I knew where my life was headed.

When I was 14 and a freshman in high school, I fell madly in love with my friend's brother. He was a star football player and I begged Maxine to get me a date with him. The summer after my freshman year he finally took me out to the drive-in theater. I wore my white angora sweater and a very tight skirt. I thought I looked Sophia Loren sexy and I was, but he didn't even kiss me. It was a mercy date. I felt like a failure for months after.

When I recovered from the rejection, I began to focus on selective dating: only cute boys who played football and were smart. The added advantage to dating was that each high school boyfriend was a further opportunity to explore the forbidden area of sex: French kissing, hand on top of breast, but only on the outside, no penis grab, nothing below the waist. I always wanted to go all the way, but I didn't know anyone who did that and I didn't want to look stupid and racy.

I discovered jazz at 15 and never looked back. First albums were John Lewis' *European Windows* and Coltrane's *My Favorite Things*. Parties were always at my house because I had a first rate playroom and the best parents. Everyone liked my father because he was cool in areas where lots of other parents were prudish. We danced, swam and played spin the bottle. Later when there was conspicuous consumption of alcohol and throwing up on the gravel driveway, Dad took the antics of teenagers in stride. He was young once, too.

Most weekends we drove to San Francisco, walked around North Beach, drank coffee at Enrico's, stood outside Basin Street West to listen to jazz and hung out at Lawrence Ferlinghetti's City Lights Book Store. We wore black turtleneck sweaters, black skirts, leggings, and black berets. We were beatniks. On the way home we hit the beach or parked under the Golden Gate Bridge and made out. The boys drank beer. I never had a curfew. My mother trusted me to do the right thing and I did. She was raising me to make good decisions for myself. That was a huge confidence builder during high school.

Catholic school provided a traditional education and we had an active drama club. We also had a solid speech class with Father Cummins as our leader. He was a handsome man, charming and smart and his students were devoted. It was one of the few classes where the boys and girls mixed; the other was typing. We had a very smart group of speech students, but I was the star from the beginning.

From the time I was 6, I knew I wanted to be an actress and that desire translated into speech competitions. I ended up winning every state speech contest in California. I was kind of famous. Father Cummins was my mentor all through high school. He gave me the confidence to be myself and made me strong and wise beyond my age.

In my junior year, I announced to Father Ben, as we lovingly called him, that I wanted to be a nun. "Why" he asked incredulously? I told him that I wanted to save the pagan babies in Africa. He paused for what seemed an eternity, smiled and said, "Why don't you go to college first, Joan. You've got plenty of time to decide after that." Father Ben later had the privledge of marrying me to a Jew. I mean, I really was teacher's pet.

In our senior year, we had a sex and marriage course. That's when I began to separate from the Catholic pack. The priest was talking about birth control/rhythm method and I stood up and asked, "If you don't want to or can't afford to have a child, what's wrong with using birth control?" Everyone knew the rhythm method wasn't effective, but there were rules and dogma we had to follow. I guess I wasn't so Catholic after all because I was convinced that I would never have children unless I wanted them or could afford to raise them.

Father Ben and his brother, a priest from Oakland, offered a tour to Europe to anyone who wanted to go after graduation. The highest tribute paid to Father Ben was from my mother who leapt at the chance to tour with the brothers. She wasn't a Catholic, but just to be in their presence, she endured every church and cathedral in 13 countries, walking through Fatima, Lourdes and almost fainting at the shroud of Christ in Turin. She soldiered on, but never missed a chance to tell me how there was no good reason for that ridiculous church I followed. My father just laughed. He wasn't really a good Catholic. He was Irish and they make their own rules.

After graduating from high school, I chose UCLA to study theater arts, however, I discovered there weren't enough theater classes to stimulate me. Besides, Berkeley in the 60s was calling me.

Before I left I did manage to lose my virginity to a gorgeous hunk I asked to do the deed. In a motel in Manhattan Beach, Jan. 1st, 1963, sex was no longer a mystery.

During the summer after my freshman year my mother walked into my room and sat down on my bed. I was reading a trashy novel. She looked serious and I was scared she disapproved of what I was reading.

"Your grandmother was Jewish."

"What does that make you?" I asked.

"Nothing. I'm nothing."

"Why are you telling me this now? You let me be raised a Catholic. That doesn't seem fair."

"It was your father's idea. What's important is that you are dating a Jewish boy."

"I am? Really? Who?"

"Peter Solomon at Draper," she said as a matter of fact. "He's rich. And he has a Jewish last name. But I wouldn't know much about it."

My mother was a treasure. An anti-semitic-semitic. Who knew? She married an Irish Catholic to hide her identity. I wasn't particularly bewildered at the idea that I was actually a Jewess. I think I always knew it. You get hunches in life – like wanting to hang out with the Jewish fraternity and only liking Jewish boys. I always held a belief that self-knowledge made you strong and following your intuition made you smart.

A year and a half later at 19, I fell in love and married a Jew to right the wrongs of my mother's disregard for her religion. We had two marriage ceremonies – one for the Catholics and one for the non-Catholics and Jews. During the first marriage ceremony inside Mission San Rafael, my almost husband, whispered, "You owe me one!"

I hope Father Ben didn't hear that. He mercifully didn't require my almost husband to take religious lessons and promise to raise his kids as Catholic. That would never have happened anyway. In retrospect that was not a good start to a marriage and probably not the best decision I could have made at 19.

Soon after my two marriage ceremonies, my husband told me he wanted to practice law in Las Vegas. Reluctantly, I picked myself up and drove to Las Vegas to start a life with a man I hardly knew. Life is always an adventure.

A few months later I was sitting in a chair in front of the president of the Sahara Hotel – probably a mob guy – in a hot, crowded office with execs and secretaries lining the walls interviewing for a job.

I walked inside wearing a summer polka-dot dress with a plunging frilly neckline that stuck to my body like glue. The president was studying my thin résumé and my thin dress. No one was sweating but me.

"So you're an actress. Recite some Shakespeare." I was ready to break out in "All the world's a stage…" when I suddenly switched to "Alas poor Yoric, I knew him well." (Yoric and I had a lot in common, but in this instance, I was the one dying.)

I stood up with my dress clinging to my back – ass-crack clearly defined – and thanked the president for his time. I took in his spinster secretary's deadly stare. I got the job at the Sahara Hotel but my real journey was just beginning.

Those early experiences gave me belief in myself, the idea that life was a series of changes, curves and surprises and to always hop on the merry-go-round. I grew up without fear and that is still my strength. I was always focused and determined about what I wanted and didn't let go until I was ready. Careers may change, circumstances may change, but the truth of who you are never changes.

I'm still little funny face Joanie Moran with the chipped front tooth from St. Raphael's Grammar School who is living a great life.

VULNERABILITY AND THE ART OF FAMILY MAINTENANCE

While walking the dogs with my daughter-in-law on our family's winter ski vacation, we found ourselves in a discussion of the 3 most serious stressors in life. In the freezing afternoon, as the sun and the barometer were dipping, Carli and I were trying to be objective about our family dynamic and the oftentimes dysfunctional nature of the marriages between my sons and their wives and between me and my sons.

"You know the three biggest stressors in life, don't you?" she asked.

"I think so," I replied, "money, divorce and change."

"You're close: finances, sex and family," Carli said to me. She is a psychologist and has the ability to pinpoint dysfunction in a flash.

Of course, I know what Carli proffered was true, but I don't always pay attention to what creates stress, chaos and drama while I'm in the middle of an uncomfortable conversation. The last thing I'm thinking about is the psychology of human behavior as it relates to anger and nasty exchanges. Only later I might recognize the emotional outbursts as a symptom of larger issues in the collective unconscious.

Stressor issues are difficult to deal with because their origin is usually fear of the unknown – the endless money/budget rabbit hole battles, the need for intimacy in relationships and how families interrelate with blame and shame.

Even if you don't have children or are not married, you still have the problem of how to handle your emotional dynamic and possible change of circumstance and behavior. No one escapes life's internal struggles. Fear is a constant in the human condition. "Humans are all about protecting, even hiding, feelings and embarrassments instead of focusing on being emotionally openly honest," I said to Carli. "Vulnerability is hard to come by naturally. No one wants to be exposed."

"Like this week," she said, "with all of us dealing with daily realities and unrealistic expectations of how everyone is behaving on the ski vacation. We all had the opportunity to be vulnerable. Some were honest about it and some were not."

I mused about my conversation with Carli and considered two techniques that might help me be more artful in my family vulnerabilities and, hopefully, reduce family stress:

1   *The 10% Solution – Step Back*
    Everyone has experienced uncomfortable discussions with family, friends or co-workers when all you want to do is get the better of someone, be right or wage the battle for no good reason other than ego.

    A good technique is to step back from the situation that involves the conflict and assess what is really happening. I call this the 10% solution. Usually, we are 100% emotionally involved in the situation that involves change or conflict. The ego takes over and wreaks havoc. Stepping away from the situation – about 10% is a good ratio – allows emotions to cool and lets the heart become the healer.

My sons and I have an unspoken rule about conflicts that arise between us. We either walk away from each other or hang up the phone. When my son and I agree to reconnect, the anger and resentment have subsided, and as my father used to say, we proceed with cooler heads.

2 *Avoid The Trigger Effect*

Most of my dysfunctional moments arise from negative past experiences that trigger my present angst. There are certain struggles in life that are difficult to put to rest. Although I believe I've moved through them, there still remain unconscious residuals of hurtful memories, and the hurt inevitably returns in times of stress. If I can mindfully separate the past from the present with conscious honesty and clear intention, I can avoid emotional triggers. That's when I can allow my vulnerabilities to exist in tandem with the discomforts. And that's when I am able to act with consciousness, empathy, sympathy, and generosity of spirit.

The moment you become emotionally honest you are more conscious of listening and understanding. Once your defensive armor has been removed, you can bring choice, strength and opportunity to the stressors of life and better understand family dynamics.

ARE WE HAVING FUN YET?

How many times have you been invited to lunch, or dinner, to a club or to the movies with high expectations about what will happen? How fun it will be! Getting together with the girls or in a mixed group will be a blast! Even meeting new people will be amazing.

Then, at some point in the middle of the gathering, the people and the place turned out to be a disappointment and you can't understand what went wrong. You thought you were going to have a great time, have fun, and be light and breezily conversant, but the party never got started for you.

Were you too worried about everything? Did you have a pre-plan in mind and it didn't turn out the way you wanted? Were your expectations too high? Were you focusing on what should happen instead on what was happening? Was your negative energy seeping through your stylish dress, your 4-inch heels and perfect Mac makeup?

We've all had the idea that having fun is simply retail bliss. Fun can be had for the purchase of the right clothing, shoes and jewelry and perfectly plucked eyebrows! And yet with all this, the need to get your endorphins pumping and go with the flow of the crowd seems to have eluded you.

Instead of having fun, you were overtaken by the virus of unconscious negativity. Without even knowing it, your mind was sending out negative thoughts and feelings. How can that be? You didn't start out feeling negative and you certainly didn't expect a negative outcome.

Harboring negative feelings and outcomes is a very common way of coping with life. It can be a default position. If you find yourself trying to have fun and not succeeding or not relating in a positive manner, it might be a moment to consciously assess what you are feeling in relation to what you are experiencing in the immediate present. That awareness is called emotional intelligence – it is a state of mind that gives you power to change your unconscious, negative mindset.

The battle between the negative and the positive isn't sparked by the words or actions of others. It doesn't happen because of what did or didn't happen at the party or event. Your negative reaction is fueled by your mind – a mind that unconsciously gives negativity way too much importance.

You see, but you don't really see. You pretend to feel, but your emotions do not come from a place of authenticity. Fun eludes you because your mindset, unconscious though it is, resides outside of the framework of the present.

This negative perspective on life translates into resistance and resistance is the most toxic force on the planet. It prevents you from living in the moment and connecting to the source of your real emotions – your heart.

Resistance is an unfortunate characteristic because it allows you to make excuses for not being the rock star you were meant to be. Unconscious negative messages surface: I'm too old, I'm too fat, I'm not pretty enough, smart enough. I'm too whatever it is that takes you out of the present moment and kills your fun.

How do you change this mental construct and go from the unconscious negative to the conscious positive so that you are having the best time of your life wherever you are and whatever you are doing?

One of the best techniques to enjoy life to the fullest is to consciously make a note to yourself. It's not about trying to do everything and be everything, it's about making the very best of what you have while enjoying the process of living. Most importantly, try to do life without judgment or labeling – characterizing something as good or bad. That mindset is negative and self-sabotaging.

It's always preferable to make the best use of available resources – your time, energy and efforts – and allow them to internalize positive change. Available resources include your beliefs, values, feelings, attitudes and behavior – your entire goodie basket of who you are and how you present yourself.

From a mindset of positivity, you are free to experience joy and feel the pleasures of having fun with a greater sense of authenticity, purpose and empowerment.

WHAT DOESN'T KILL YOU
What doesn't kill you makes you stronger
Stand a little taller
Doesn't mean I'm lonely when I'm alone
What doesn't kill you makes a fighter
Footsteps even lighter
- From *What Doesn't Kill You (Stronger)* sung by Kelly Clarkson

KICK BUTT EVERY DAY

I was talking to my best friend today and we both said the same thing at the same time: *Kick Butt Every Day* and give that day the best of who you are.

We were drinking our TGIF margaritas after I gave him a tango lesson, as was our usual end of the week ritual. We were talking about the methodology of our respective career trajectories. We both have hard-core work ethics, and for two former stage actors whose careers were dependent on the hustle of getting the next gig, we were pretty much on the same page in how we define showing up.

Here's how we kick butt every day. I think it's pretty cool for two people who have lived almost 7 decades.

The Gratitude Gig

Get up every day with an attitude of gratitude. Show up to the office to make your ten calls or sit in front of your computer and make an intention to write the blog that's on your mind, or work on your speech and start the day with positive energy. Negatives have no place in your world.

In order to get to a higher level of productivity, you've got to create the habit of being organized with the things you can control and let go of the things you can't. The third part of this equation is to allow the good things to come to you. It's a matter of surrendering and letting go in life. It all comes to you in time.

The Emotional Gig

Of course, managing yourself is the most essential personal and professional challenge. How you show up for life after you wake up determines the quality of that day along with its results. When you are unfocused, stressed and not present, you've got some immediate problems.

Mental chaos and mind clutter (the evil twins) allow emotions to take over. You become resistant and reactive and time gets wasted. When you live with greater focus, you act with deliberateness, and more importantly, *mindfulness*.

Mindfulness is becoming a *catch all* word today because it's ubiquitous in psychology, management and interpersonal relationships. But just because it's everywhere in our culture, it doesn't mean that mindfulness is a less powerful self-management tool.

You may have noticed that your personal and professional life isn't working very well with that multi-tasking behavior. Multi-tasking is a habit you should lose because it promotes chaos instead of awesome results. Mindset experts tell us that multi-tasking is a misnomer. It's just not humanly possible to do a bunch of things at the same time with any amount of expertise.

The Balance Gig

When you want to kick butt in the morning, a crucial skill set is managing your emotional reactions (how you are feeling inside).

Unfortunately, most of us never learn the skill of balancing our mind and body very well. Educators don't teach it in school and businesses are not inclined to encourage the soft skills – your internal tools. What's noticeable, however, is that more and more leaders are setting stock in the ability to manage your inside life.

Although your nervous system is there to protect you with flight or fight, most of the time your emotions simply freeze up when the going gets tough – you've got a big meeting ahead of you and panic sets in. You can do a lot of damage to your physical and mental health when your life is unbalanced.

Wouldn't it be a huge plus to develop mindfulness in keeping our emotional responses in balance? It might save a lot of useless conflict.

The Meditation Gig

My major intention with my best friend was to get him to do a 10-minute meditation before he starts his day. Years later, he absolutely believes in that quiet time before he looks at a paper or picks up the phone.

My friend told me that he is more able to see what's around him, feel the joys of engaging fully with people, places and things and has reduced the negativity that once plagued him.

All humans are inherently fearful. And fears come up at the most inopportune moments during the day. If you stay present, you are much more likely to acknowledge your fears and treat them as your most valuable possessions.

And then you can really kick butt.

IT'S YOUR SHIP: EMOTIONAL INTELLIGENCE RULES!

In the long line of to-dos and *psychological buzzwords, must haves* and *shoulds,* we are now exploring something called *emotional intelligence.* Did some psychologist make this up or is it for real?

The theory of multiple intelligences has garnered a wide variety of interest in recent decades. Harold Gardner, an American developmental psychologist, speculates in his 1983 book, *Frames of Mind: The Theory of Multiple Intelligences,* articulated eight criteria for a behavior to be considered an intelligence. Gardner chose eight abilities that meet this criteria: musical/rhythmic, visual/spatial, verbal/linguistic, logical/mathematical, bodily/kinesthetic, interpersonal, intrapersonal, and naturalistic. He later suggested that existential and moral intelligence might also be worthy of inclusion.

Daniel Goleman, psychologist and author of the book, *Emotional Intelligence,* created another category called emotional intelligence – the ability to recognize our emotional landscape and deal with it using an array of skills and characteristics that drive leadership performance.

I decided to delve into emotional intelligence after a trip to New Orleans last November. I sat next to a man who was a project manager in northern California. Since I was about to embark on writing a speech about business leadership, I asked him what he thought were the best practices for managing a business. He advised me to read a book called, *It's Your Ship*, by Captain D. Michael Abrashoff. The subtitle was even more intriguing: *Management Techniques from the Best Damn Ship in the Navy.*

It's Your Ship

Captain Abrashoff assumed command of a ship that was rated the worst in the Navy. He believed that human beings are the capital of a ship, just as individuals are the capital of a corporation. In two years, the Captain's ship was on the cutting-edge of ship performance and productivity. It was rated #1 in the Navy.

Within months of taking command, Captain Abrashoff got to know every sailor aboard the ship. He knew the talents of each individual crew member, found sailors who wanted to lead by example and challenged everyone to be the best they could be at their job. Because the Captain knew everything about his crew, including birthdays, the number of children and when babies were born, he inspired loyalty, trust and happiness on board. The Captain's slogan was: *It's Your Ship!*

It's Your Life

According to Daniel Goldman, author of *Emotional Intelligence: Why It Can Matter More Than IQ,* Captain Abrashoff's empathic response is a form of emotional intelligence – the ability to manage and reflect the emotions of others and of self.

Emotional intelligence is not just a management skill, but also a necessary life skill for creating strong and committed interpersonal relationships leading to greater happiness.

Dr. Goldman suggests that emotional intelligence is linked to everything from decision-making to academic achievement and also has an impact on children's developmental learning. The study of emotional intelligence has paved the way for a slew of business tools, indicating a paradigm shift from the importance of hard tools to the necessity of implementing soft tools worldwide.

It's annoying and frustrating when feelings, disappointments, frustrations and sadness are not acknowledged or are not reflected back to you. Telling your best friend, your lover, your mother how you are feeling and finding an empathic response not forthcoming makes you feel worse or even angry.

Why aren't your feelings being reflected back to you in your husband's supportive words or hugs? Where is your father's warm and loving reply to your sadness? Where is that supportive embrace and concern for real communication from your lover? You want someone to listen, someone to feel what you feel with mindfulness and connection.

Conversation, the give-and-take of energy, fires up the neurotransmitters and keeps people mindful of the contextual involvement. That conscious awareness leads to a greater collective feeling of happiness. Emotionally intelligent people understand intuitively what emotions are being expressed and being felt. Being fully conscious and aware of what's going on inside gives strength to your outside actions.

You've seen how some people are completely clueless in social situations. They look out of their element. They give obvious signs that they are not connecting to the situation – eyes dart around, the body is fidgeting and restless and they add nothing to the conversation. If they realize anything, it's that they are not participating. They feel isolated and they usually walk away.

However, emotionally intelligent people connect in social situations by reacting in a positive manner to the emotions of other people. They have the ability to manage the contextual energy in the present.

What makes emotionally intelligent people so awesome is not only that they understand the dynamics of others, but they also have the ability to empathize, improving the quality of their relationships based on appropriate feedback about the needs of others. Emotionally intelligent people live a happier and more fulfilling life because they power up their emotional antenna and pay closer attention to their surroundings and how they fit into a social circle.

And what's even more amazing is that it's possible to learn the emotional communication skills necessary for establishing, maintaining, and deepening relationships *at any age*. This is a strong component of successful people as well as successful businesses.

Three cheers to Captain Abrashoff for giving us an excellent example of how the skill set of emotionally intelligent people provide personal and professional leadership.

"The greater part of human pain is unnecessary. It is self-created as long as the unobserved mind runs your life." ~Eckhart Tolle

When I came across Eckhart Tolle's quote, I was reminded how profound and influential Mr. Tolle has been in encouraging modern culture to embrace *the power of* now, which is also the title of his book. Tolle encourages the idea of staying 100% in the present moment and to be mindful in thought and action to avoid human pain. The past is over and the future is an illusion.

Which mind runs your life, the unobserved, unconscious mind or the conscious present mind?

The unobserved, unconscious mind runs amok with mindless mental chatter. You're like a 5-year-old who is running on sugar and, therefore, running on empty. I used to be over-stimulated when I walked through the door of a party that's already in progress. At one particular New Year's Eve party in the Hollywood Hills in Los Angeles, I got lost in the hills and arrived later than I would have liked. Everyone was eating and drinking and talking loudly.

I couldn't focus on meeting anyone at the party and I began to be fearful that I wasn't going to connect with anyone. I even found myself feeling no connection to myself and I wandered around, grazing at the food table, but unable to eat. I felt as if I was in a nightmare and couldn't get out. I finally walked out of the party well before midnight without saying hello or goodbye to anyone. It was a lonely drive home on a crowded Sunset Blvd.

The next morning, awake with a clear head and a conscious mind, I was able to explore a profound learning experience from the previous night. I didn't want to be alone on New Year's Eve and I went to a strange place with people I didn't know and expected to celebrate because I didn't want to be alone. In fact, I was alone!

What you choose to think about and how you choose to behave is your choice. Your choice is important because it acknowledges that you are willing to take personal responsibility for your happiness, for your destiny and for reaching your human potential. It starts with accepting and surrendering to your feelings and the fears resulting from being uncomfortable, rejected, criticized, ridiculed or ignored.

Fear prevents you from assuming responsibility for your thoughts and actions. It's relatively easy to give in to fear because fear translates into *resistance.*

Fear will keep you from action but fascination won't let you walk away.

In theory, you know that some fears are irrational. Then why are you fearful? Perhaps fear is a recognition that might create artificial boundaries allowing you to stay in a familiar place.

It's common knowledge that some degree of fear is healthy because your body's built-in defense mechanism keeps you safe from harm. However, when fear becomes a barrier that prevents you from growing and transforming your life, it is clear that fear is connected to everything that controls positive decisions and truthful behavior.

Feel the fear and don't run away from it; and then go and do what you fear.

Whenever I am fearful, I ask myself that all encompassing question:

What's the worst that can happen?

I try to imagine what would be the worst possible outcome of my fears and *write it down.* Not only does admitting fear lessen the impact, but writing it down also makes your mind more analytical.

I have a friend who wants to start dating online, but has spent the better part of two years avoiding putting a profile up online. He wants a relationship, but he is unconsciously fearful of going out and meeting women. His fear of rejection overrides his desires and needs.

I ask him: What's the worst that can happen? Heartbreak? Who hasn't had heartbreak, but you don't die of heartbreak. Yet, I think my friend's fear goes deeper: What if he finds a woman that he could possibly fall in love with? What then? Perhaps he is afraid his dreams will come true, and then he has to suddenly be in a relationship with all its attendant compromises.

You might see how you've made your story fit a fantasy conclusion. Writing down your fears can give you insight into what causes anxious feelings. As you begin to recognize your fear for what it is – *imaginary anxiety* - give it a name, like Tootsie or Fred. Then make Tootsie or Fred your friend and not your fear, not your enemy.

The idea that you don't demonize your fears reminds me of a rebound boyfriend that I ran into several months after he dumped me. I was afraid to confront him at a tango festival. I knew he was there because he wanted to talk to me, but I didn't want to see him or talk to him. When I did talk to him, I was so full of fear that I made a mess of the encounter. Later, when I saw him again and he wanted to talk more, my fear overcame me again and I lashed out with fear once again.

How simple would it have been if I confronted my imaginary fear related to rejection and written out my version of the worst that could happen? I could have assessed the situation for what it was and embraced my fear.

My favorite expression lately is:

Darling, I'm sick of your story.

How many times do I have to hear the same sob story about your boyfriend that took off in the middle of the night, your lady friend who rages at you for not recycling or how you wish you could get another job? This is another way fear manifests itself in your life.

"If he/she doesn't love me anymore, what am I going to do?" This kind of self-talk distorts your feelings. It's made up, unfounded anxiety. It's negative thinking caused by run-away imagination. Shift your mindset away from fears to positive outcomes.

When managing your fears, uncontrolled imagination can be your adversary. When you are daydreaming, when you are mindlessly thinking about your own struggles with life, your imagination can run amuck. A technique to control your story about your fear is to journal. Journaling tracks your story and gives you an opportunity to change it.

Title your story and create dialogue between you and your fears. Use your values, beliefs and vulnerabilities to guide you along the path of emotional, social and spiritual health. As long as you keep telling your same old story, fear will reside within.

Breathe through your fears and see how it goes from there. As your breath becomes deeper, you are more able to control fears and anxieties. Deep breathing reaches down into the body's core, reduces stress and relaxes your mind. You will find yourself squarely in the present moment.

And remember: Respect yourself enough to walk away from anything that no longer serves you, grows you, or makes you happy.

VULNERABILITY: THE KEY TO LIVING WELL

I was driving to UCLA on my way to teach a yoga class and I wasn't feeling like myself. It was a strange and wonderful feeling. "What's up with me," I asked myself? Who is this woman driving slowly down Sunset to the Wooden Center? She usually drives like a bat out of hell.

I immediately thought: "Wow! I'm feeling so grateful for my life, my family, my gifts, my friends, my opportunities and all my successes and failures. That's who I am today. It's a good feeling." After that a few moments, I realized, suddenly, that I can name my feeling – JOY. Pure joy! I had no defensive barriers at that moment; my mind wasn't running amuck. I was clear and I was present. I was conscious and had no need of self-protective defensive mechanisms.

I heard Dr. Brene Brown give a TEDTalk on the topic of vulnerability. Dr. Brown is a research professor at the University of Houston Graduate College of Social Work. She has been studying shame, fear, and vulnerability for 12 years. From her research and study, Dr. Brown posits that vulnerability holds the key to emotional intimacy, overcoming shame and releasing your creative powers.

She made the point that to be vulnerable is to have real strength and not just the old-fashioned muscle strength. From personal experience, Dr. Brown related that getting in touch with her extensive emotional palate allowed her to realize a more creative and fulfilling life.

What's the big deal about accepting our vulnerability? Being vulnerable isn't that tragic. It would be worse to live out real tragedy in a Shakespearean play or even worse to find yourself in a Woody Allen melodrama. Now that's tragic!

Being vulnerable is about being emotionally openly honest and that involves embracing your own emotions, accepting them and surrendering to them. They are part and parcel of your being, your nature and part of what gives you strength and conviction in life.

How do we surrender to being emotionally openly honest? Is there a secret formula?

Here is the secret: If you want to live a healthy, fulfilling and joyful life, if you want to live a creative life that allows for an open mind, a soaring imagination that is open to new and exciting ideas, be vulnerable and acknowledge your extensive emotional palate.

Of course, it's a challenging journey because you are connecting to the unconscious – the hidden secrets of your soul, your innermost being, and your dream landscape. This is the path to acknowledging and observing your *shadow self* – the person we think we know, the person we are mindfully more comfortable with – the most significant and magnificent part of your amazing self.

Face it: human nature being what it is, we are tentative and afraid of the unknown. OMG! What's behind that decision we are making? What's going to happen to me if I choose X or Y? I've got to know the outcome before the decision making process starts otherwise all hell will break loose.

Admittedly, being vulnerable is sometimes a scary place to be. Why leave a perfectly satisfying comfort zone when being authentic can be intimidating? You don't know what's on the other side of you.

In a profound sense, embracing vulnerability is the path to creativity and to living a joyful and fulfilling life. By acknowledging your emotions, you give yourself permission to live your life to the fullest and that's a pretty cool place to be because *your vulnerable self is the source of your real power.*

Everything you feel, every emotion you express is another step closer to self-knowledge and to living well. That's why my beautiful moment of joy driving to UCLA and my yoga classes was so profound. I felt openly, emotionally honest, living without fear and expectation. I was living in the middle of an abundant life.

STAYING ALIVE

Life goin' nowhere, somebody help me
Somebody help me, yeah
Life goin' nowhere, somebody help me, yeah
I'm stayin' alive
- From *Staying Alive* sung by The Bee Gees

....

STAYING ALIVE, STAYING ALIVE

Life doesn't have to be perfect to be wonderful. The possibility of creating a successful life that is balanced and blissful keeps options and opportunities alive so we can grow and change.

To create a successful life also means being comfortable with who you are and who you want to become. It's that magic time when what you want and what you have match up. It's like an eclipse of the sun, but the magic time lasts longer than 7 minutes and 31 seconds.

When you create a successful life, you seize the moment, like eating pizza in bed at midnight watching *Casablanca* or dancing around your living room in your underwear to the Bee Gees' *Staying Alive, Staying Alive* or doing an imaginary poll dance to Whitney Houston's *Let's Dance*.

For your life to be fulfilling and blissful, it's important to be mindful of all your decisions and choices. It's mind boggling how we let distractions and mindless messages from our environment overtake our conscious awareness and keep us from making great decisions – instead meeting dead ends.

I don't want dead ends and I know you don't either!

So think of staying alive this way:

The Future Of Your Life Is Purpose because the act of living requires purpose, a determination or a design that gives meaning and energy to life. Finding purpose with self-awareness is one of the most important ways that the mind develop clear intention. My mother always used to say to me, "Joanie, you're a born teacher. So teach." And I've been teaching since I was 22 years old. Teaching is the gift that keeps on giving because it manifests the purpose of my life. It leads me to learning and knowing experiences. Teaching helps me keep my commitment strong to honor my life and my work.

Give Value to Your Family and Community and it will inspire and motivate the people in your life to share your values, and therefore, your message. This is the law of the mind in action and the key to maximizing your human potential and living a successful life. In a profound sense, giving value to your family and community gives you the opportunity to find purpose in your life.

Trust Your Heart because your heart doesn't lie. Your mind lies. The heart is an energy center that always leads to a successful life. It is the center of a generosity of spirit, a place of true forgiveness and the center of all your happiness and personal success. The heart prevents you from getting caught up in needless drama, people, places and things that get in the way of your clear intention. Listen to your heart first and let the mind follow.

Believe in yourself and you are on the path to a successful life. Believing in yourself means trusting the truth of your path – your dharma – that is the truth of your journey. It is only then that you can live a fulfilling, productive, joyful and successful life.

How does life get so complicated? How do you find yourself with so much dead weight? The externals, money, things and a gaggle of friends are never the barometer of success. The need to acquire material things at a certain age might be appealing, but when the focus shifts to acquiring less, real life kicks in.

So live simply and live well and embrace a world that looks different, feels different, and thinks different.

We exert a lot of effort making decisions not just in our daily lives, but also in our work lives. Have you ever counted how many decisions we make in a day? That may be a good exercise because we make probably well over a couple hundred.

Sometimes it seems like a real struggle to make even the smallest of decisions. Should you go to the bank today, should you buy those long overdo tennis shoes because your feet are really hurting, should you take Sunset or Wilshire to West Hollywood, what yoga outfit should you wear this morning, what should you eat for breakfast, lunch or dinner, what flight should you take, what time should you leave for the airport, what blog should you write, when should you work on your business proposal?

By the end of the day, decision-making has exhausted you – and these are just the mundane decisions that get you through an hour at a time. What about the most important decisions in life – the decisions that are more profound, the decisions that improve the quality of your life, affect your path, your journey, your dharma (truth), your human potential, growth and perhaps even your transformation?

Effective decision-making comes from a strong intention to integrate mind, body and spirit (energy) into a well-balanced individual with unlimited potential for personal and professional growth.

Acknowledging this connectivity will not only bridge the mind/body gap, but also provide an essential transitional step that improves self-worth and confidence.

Your brain is usually way too cluttered with ideas and emotions. This monkey mind, chatty and unfocused, keeps the synapses moving so fast across the brain that it never gets a chance to catch up with itself. It feels like you are off balance because you can't slow the mind down.

More often than not, I don't know when I'm out of balance. The only way I know is that something feels wrong. I am "out of sorts."

My mind/body/spirit connection is lost and I feel stuck in my thinking and my intentions are not clear. I don't know what to do next.

What is really happening is that my thoughts pour out in an endless loop – a mindless loop and I cannot for the life of me quiet my mind. It takes time to get rid of the noise inside my head. At these moments, I make an intention to let go of my thoughts as they come tumbling out of my mind. I then try to find space in my brain that allows me to make decisions with less struggle and better outcomes (See the movie *What The Bleep Do We Know*).

How do you change the mind-numbing habit of chaotic thinking so you see more clearly and make decisions that are intention driven rather than "shooting from the hip," which produces mindless chaos?

A smart way to begin the journey is to take some time to reflect and set aside some old mindsets, rigid ideas and limited perceptions. We know that a closed mind, a mind that clings and restricts, allows us to compartmentalize past and future thinking. That's a prescription for mindless repetition and repetition can be a real brain killer.

To change is to challenge some of the persistent struggles you encounter daily as a result of unclear thinking. Begin to see your life in terms of process and not outcomes or goals. Intentions are immediate and more manageable.

Maybe you'll break a habit, eliminate something superfluous in your life, do something that makes you feel insecure, strange, scary, or carry out an action with complete intensity and attention as if it was your last. Think outside the box, no, think inside the box where you may have overlooked a fabulous idea.

The results will be stunning. The mindful choices you make today will enhance the quality of your life, deepen your ability to assess your individual needs and guide you to think in multiple perspectives in a variety of contexts. You will be more inspired, more energized, and more mindful of all aspects of your life and work.

By connecting your mind and body and spirit and pursuing the path of maximizing your potential, you'll be able to imagine a universe that thinks

different, looks different, and feels different. I'm in for that.

....

LIVE WHAT YOU BELIEVE

I decided long ago, never to walk in anyone's shadows
If I fail, if I succeed
At least I'll live as I believe
No matter what they take from me
They can't take away my dignity
- From *The Greatest Love of All* sung by Whitney Houston

....

WAKE UP POSITIVE EVERY DAY AND STAY STRONG

Have you ever spent a night in fitful sleep, disturbing dreams or awakened at 3 a.m. with a mind so active you had to take a sleeping pill? Or are those redundant questions?

Oh, yes, you've been there. The thought of getting up is a real downer. You try to roll out of bed with a dry mouth and a body that does not want to move in any direction. Sitting up takes way too much effort.

Is this any way to greet the world? Is this your best face, your sharpest mind or your most presentable body? You feel like the Ogre in the movie *Shrek*. Grumpy describes your attitude and that's not a good look.

How could you feel any other way? There was unfinished business at the office yesterday, a relationship that is on the rocks, children not doing their homework or a PTA meeting that you really don't want to attend. There is soccer practice, a piano recital and your resolve to get to the gym is thwarted by a lunch meeting the boss called. Sounds like a prescription to go back to bed.

Here are 20 ways to wake up positive and stay happy, stress free and energized with creative fervor all day every day.

1 Don't Move A Muscle
Lie still. Ease into the present slowly. Let your mind and body connect without jarring movements.

2 Relax Your Body
It's natural when you first wake up to think you feel relaxed, but you might not actually be relaxed. We tense up at night and we might still be tense when we begin to wake up. Consciously bring your body to a state of complete relaxation.

3 Try to Remember Your Dreams
Most people will say they cannot remember their dreams or that they don't dream at all. We all dream multiple times during the night. You can train your mind to remember your dreams by lying absolutely still without thought when you first wake up. Dreams reflect our unconscious feelings. It's worth paying attention to your unconscious emotional state. You might be enlightened.

4 Meditate
Waking up the body is different for everyone, but a great way to enter the present is with an intention to meditate. If thoughts are running amok, try to clear your mind. Slowly roll out of bed

and sit on a pillow, back against the wall and spend time (at the beginning 2 – 5 minutes) sitting quietly letting your thoughts go.

5 Align Your Energy
A straight spine is essential for meditating because energy can move through your body unobstructed. Shrug your shoulders back and feel your sit bones rooting. Note your body's stillness.

6 Focus On Breathing
Find your breath interesting. After all, breathing is the essential ingredient for staying alive. It is your life force so honor it with attention.

7 Consider What Makes You Happy
Choose 3 things that make you happy. Turn up the corners of your mouth into a big smile. Your happy thoughts will be forefront in your consciousness all day.

8 Have An Attitude of Gratitude
Your inner clock will begin to nudge you. It's at this moment that you begin the gratitude phase of waking up: name 5 things you are grateful for and smile.

9 Get Rid of the Negative
Having negative thoughts at the beginning of your day is a risk to your well being. Your brain wants to go into negative mode first. It's human nature to dwell on the negative. Resist it and shift focus to what is positive about your day and your life.

10 Don't Attach
Don't attach to thoughts when you wake up. You've got the whole day to do that. Attachment fosters illusion rather than reality and causes stress and anxiety.

11 Think Yes Instead of No

No means resistance is at work. *Yes* means possibilities and opportunities are before you. Put your finger on *Yes*. Be strong and willing to cross over a mental threshold and be surprised.

12 Stay Present

Make an intention to stay present during the day. If you think future or past thoughts, reconnect with the present moment. The power of the day is in the now.

13 Eliminate Something From Your Day

Make an intention to eliminate something superfluous from your day. Make it a practice to give up something daily. Non-attachment is good for the soul.

14 Be With Happy People

Make an intention to surround yourself with joyful, happy people during the day. Walk away from energy drains – people, places and things that stand in the way of your happiness and keep you stuck in the quicksand of the day.

15 Take On Positive Pursuits

Invest in positive pursuits during the day. Keep the negatives away. If you are lacking in positive energy, negative energy will pursue you. Do something that brings joy into your life. Go to the gym, eat a healthy lunch or call someone and acknowledge the gift of that person's friendship.

16 Stay Off of One Social Media A Day

Eliminate one social media outlet a day. Stay off Facebook or Twitter and rely on your own energy to keep you positive.

17 Be Mindful At All Times

Take time for self-reflection. Assess how you feel inside yourself. Self-reflection is like taking your emotional and spiritual temperature. You don't need to know how things work or understand the meaning of life. Live it.

18 Give No Excuses, No Blame

It's human nature to make excuses and to apply blame when things are not going well. Make an intention to take full responsibility for what you do every day.

19 Embrace Daily Challenges

Life is an opportunity – an opportunity to be the best that you can be. If you are thirsty, drink, if you are hungry, eat. Every thing you do has meaning and purpose and affects your creativity.

20 Exercise

Daily exercise promotes positive attitudes. Your neurotransmitters will be on fire all day. Exercise in the morning – that morning walk is also meditative – noontime or evening. Do at least 20 minutes daily for good heart health.

Dive into the day with positive energy and full consciousness and greet your day as a gift to cherish. Your life will take on new meaning by staying positive.

THE FORCE BE WITH YOU
You can bend but never break me
'Cause it only serves to make me
More determined to achieve my final goal
And I come back even stronger
Not a novice any longer
- From *The Force Be With You* sung by Helen Reddy

. . . .

EAT, DRINK, BREATHE: HEALTHY HABITS TO KEEP YOU
STRONG

I've been interested in health and wellness since my mother forced me to eat overcooked broccoli and soggy squash when I was 6 years old. My mother was a home economist with her heart in the right place, but there had to be food that tasted better than what my mother cooked – although my sons tell me that my food is as bland as their Grandma's.

We've thankfully evolved our knowledge of what constitutes healthy eating and cooking over the decades, including the ubiquitous vegetarian diet, the somewhat popular vegan possibilities (no dairy or meat, chicken or fish) and lesser popular choice of eating raw on a full-time basis (my favorite – call me crazy).

My choice to go vegetarian in 1971 was dictated more by my first pregnancy than by any spiritual philosophy. For 9 months, I had constant gas pain, bloat and heartburn. I wasn't concerned with how cows or chickens were slaughtered or how fish suffered at the end of a pole or inside a net. How could I think about animal cruelty when I was doubled over on the floor writhing in my own pain?

I made an amateur medical diagnosis about how I was feeling and cut out foods that played havoc with my digestive system. I stuck to soft foods and thanks to green plants and fruits; I got my protein and increased my energy. Becoming a vegan wasn't a thought in my universe. Who gives up dairy anyway? I loved my eggs and yoghurt.

Yet, my eating has evolved over time. Today I eat almost the same thing every day and I eat small portions. Friends tease me unmercifully for my food choices and my sons ask me if I want birdseed with my fruit.

A decade ago, I began to eat chicken again, but this time, the visual of how they are caged and slaughtered not only freaked me out, but was also out of step with my spiritual path. I never returned to beef, not even my favorite T-bone steak. It brings back memories of heartburn.

During the past several years, I eliminated all but an occasional sushi outing and a nice piece of fish for old times sake. I always think I need to eat wild salmon for the omega 3s crusaders (health food junkies and nutritionists), but I realize I get plenty of fish oil in everything else and dairy in my latte. Can't give up that!

Here's my mostly raw diet:

Fruit in the morning is a must for me. I usually eat a banana and a couple of handfuls of berries. I also take a multi-vitamin that has everything else I might need to complete a day full of health.

A green drink a day either in the morning or mid-afternoon: kale, spinach, beets, carrots, bananas, goji berries, flaxseed, chia and hemp seeds, Persian cucumbers, strawberries, pineapple, maybe blueberries or peaches, lemon, or ginger. I love the repetitive cutting and chopping motions. I add a powder – organic barley grass juice powder (you can also add extra protein powder) or Matcha, a green tea extract. The creative process of building my green drink is truly a meditation and a surprise.

An apple a day in mid or late afternoon has been a favorite of mine since I can remember. I put peanut butter on it – that's how I get my portion of nuts during the day. But you have to love peanut butter – otherwise, just eat it plain. It's refreshing and full of fiber.

Nuts are underrated as nutritious snacks — particularly raw tree nuts, such as almonds, cashews, walnuts, and more, which have been linked to lower cholesterol, better heart health, weight control and even a lower cancer risk.

Green salad finishes my day. In addition to more kale and spinach, I add what looks good on the salad bar – beets, carrots, legumes, hummus, peppers, and tomatoes.

The secret of good health and wellness is eating healthy. Keep the fatty foods at bay, eliminate sugar and white flour and be fairly repetitious in your daily eating habits. Most people think it's boring eating the same foods daily, but I always remember that my mind, body and spirit are nurtured by the whole foods I choose to eat. They give me all the nutrients I need to consume each day.

Remember to *breathe* when you eat. It slows down the chewing process. The last person I ate with inhaled the food and I wondered if he even tasted it. Mindful breathing helps the digestive system and as a bonus eliminates heartburn.

ANYTHING IS POSSIBLE AT ANY AGE

I was driving from Los Angeles to Austin, Texas, following the trailer that was moving the contents of my life – 45 boxes that represented the material total of 71 years of life on this planet – to a city halfway across the country. I had hoped to do the driving during daylight hours, however, Murphy's Law dictated that everything that could go wrong would go wrong with my moonlighting mover. It was too good to be true to have a smooth move on the cheap.

We got a late start and by the time we got out of Los Angeles on the 10 Freeway, it was clear to me that we would never make El Paso by 11 pm.

Saved By A Friend

You don't know how wonderful good friends can be until you really need them. We were headed toward Tucson when it dawned on me we needed to find a cheap motel to crash. I had cancelled the Super 8 in El Paso hours before. It was nearing midnight and we were all exhausted.

My friend called and asked where I was. "You'll never make El Paso. Drive through Tucson and get a motel in Benson. It's the next city." He then proceeded to recommend 4 motels that were all visible on the city's main street. Problem solved!

The drive from Los Angeles to Austin is approximately 19 hours. Sleeping adds 6 more hours (you can't sleep much anyway) and gas and restroom stops add another 7-8 hours. It's a slog no matter how you do it, but if you are pushing to get to Austin and unload boxes on day 2 of travel because the AT&T guy is coming the next morning to hook up your cable and Internet, the possibility that you'll make that deadline decreases with each mile.

I was determined – *determined* to set the move up my way and get out of Dodge by January 26th. *My mantra kicked in: Anything is possible at any age.* Age is only a number. The real age of a body is the strength of the spine. I have a spine of steel and a mind like a one-note samba.

Limping Along

In the dark terrain of the west Texas hill country, I felt like I was surrounded by a Tim Burton set design. It was scary, strange and a little ridiculous. I stepped outside myself and saw the adventurous 19-year-old girl I once was. "Hey, 19, Steely Dan," I said aloud. I suddenly felt my spine straighten, my energy ignite, my face move and my dry eyes blink.

Even though my moving plans seemed ill advised, even though I could have transported my car, and even though I was slowly killing my mover and his girlfriend, I knew we could make this drive in 2 days. I knew I could arrive no later than 11:30 p.m. and move the contents of my life into my new apartment – an apartment that I had actually never seen!

There are infinite possibilities at any age.

Falling In Love

It took a week and a half to settle in because good friends were there to help and family was there to support. I had been visiting Austin for the previous 2 ½ years so I knew I loved the city on the outside.

Although Austin's *Keep Austin Weird* slogan isn't quite accurate anymore. It's a city on the move in so many ways. It's a city with nuances, a city where music is king, dancing is high on the list of activities for all ages and possibilities abound. I even went to a Rotary club meeting in my third week and a Texas Women In Business group two days later. I teach 2 yoga classes a week in my apartment building – which, because of its beauty and friendliness feels like I'm living with greater possibilities.

I'm in love and it isn't a man that is capturing my fancy and making me flirt and smile my way through the day. It's Austin with its new buildings, east side renovations, newly arrived millennials, incredible friendliness, new restaurants with food that makes statements, endless walks around the river and biking along mountain trails cherished by the outdoor spirit that the city engenders.

Austin is an endless visual feast with so much to do that I shudder to think what would have happened to me if I had no imagination, no guts and no vision of how I wanted to live for the rest of my life.

Cheers to all the new people I have met from New York, Indiana, Chicago, Los Angeles, New Jersey and to the Austinites who chirp "y'all" with conviction. Cheers to those who have sold everything to live a life with possibilities at any age.

The truth is that no one wants to move when they are getting older because it disrupts the comfort zone It's a pain in the butt. It takes effort and courage and vision. But if you want possibilities, if you want to experience new and different things, if you want to create your life instead of just living it, if you want to fall in love, get in your covered wagon and find gold in them thar hills.

Yes, there are two paths you can go by,
but in the long run
There's still time to change the road you're on
And it makes me wonder.
- From *Stairway to Heaven* sung by Led Zeppelin

MY LATEST RETIREMENT TOUR

Cher and I have one thing in common. Along with other rock groups like The Who, Cher and I have had several final farewell retirement tours. Just like Cher, I'm on my latest but maybe not my last retirement tour. We've still got mileage.

As long as I can still do a headstand at 71, I'm good to keep on touring. Some rockers don't even have a great set of pipes left – at least I still have the strength to do a headstand.

I'm guessing that most of you in your 60s think retirement is in your future. And I'm betting that most of you still in the workforce know the exact year, month, day, and hour your Social Security kicks in.

Let's put the brakes on that retirement option right now. You are not going to retire from life, disappear into the woodwork, withdraw from society, or watch paint peel off the walls and then get ready to die are you? Not going to happen.

Walter Cronkite called retirement "statutory senility." Cher and I refuse to have any part of that and you don't have to either.

You need a new way of thinking about what I call our Act 3. From personal experience, I know that my age – 71 years old – is the most exciting time of life.

What's great about retirement tours is that they explore new and different ways to grow older, which require new and different approaches to living life to its fullest. The various incarnations of Act

3 are not about what happens to you, but about what you do with what happens to you. It's about making choices that strengthen your well being and help you realize your dreams and passions leading to greater happiness.

Today, you have more options and opportunities to create the life you deserve than you could possibly imagine. That's why I keep touring. I recently drove from Los Angeles to Austin to take up a new life. Now that's going on a real tour!

Remember when your parents retired? It seems like an ancient ritual now. That was old-school thinking. They sat in front of the TV most nights, went to bingo on Saturday or played cards with friends. Improving Dad's golf game was important and Mom could never get Dad to travel. Since they did little exercise, they had more health problems and they died earlier than they should. That's not you!

I want to respectfully encourage you to set aside the old clichéd ideas about retirement and consider taking a more meaningful journey during your 60s and for the rest of your life. Start by creating a new paradigm of how you want to live your life – not just grow older. It drives me crazy when people say they are going to retire because it's not applicable or relevant in the 21st century. There is so much to explore, so many new and creative activities to embrace.

There is support to substantiate reframing age. An AARP trends survey reported that Baby Boomers – all 76 million – are going to lead the way in how we age. Ken Dychtwald, the famous gerontologist, calls this movement *the age of transformation.*

Baby Boomers are smart and productive. We have learned how to balance our hopes and aspirations with a renewed sense of purpose. And we are definitely going to live longer because there is a new sense of freedom knocking at our door.

Maya Angelou, famous poet and author, said on the occasion of her 70th plus birthday:

"I've learned that making a living is not the same thing as making a life."

You've made a living, but have you made a life? Work is not everything because living creatively is what provides meaning and context to life.

Think of your life as a 3-act play. Acts 1 & 2 are the formative years – work and family. These early and middle years are the prelude for the best act of the play – your Act 3.

I want to challenge you to create the most awesome retirement tour imaginable. I want you to have the most amazing time in your life right now. Stay present and dance as if no one is watching. Keep the retirement tour going. Learn to do a headstand, find your passions and be grateful for all your gifts and blessings.

YOU GET BETTER AS YOU AGE

You've heard it before: *Life gets better as you age.* Really? Does it? Or is that just a fabrication of modern consumerism? Is that mantra just to get us to buy a quick fix and look ten years younger with a face lift, a pill or a personal trainer?

Maybe life doesn't actually get better as you age, but *you* certainly get better. You don't have to slow down as you get into your 60s or even 70s – I'm more energetic and *out there* than ever before. The invitation that came from AARP more than 17 years ago did not give me a rush or change my life – except that I got a senior discount at the movies.

What gives me a daily rush is that I am more in tune with myself. I'm not just another version of me; I'm doing my life through the lens of a deeper place inside of me. And from that deeper place comes an appreciation for time that is not defined, for change that is meaningful, for self-reflection that brings wisdom, understanding and grace.

Who calls the shots now? It's definitely not ambition and success, ego or activity. That was when you were young and momentum meant everything. It was an anathema to stop, sit, watch and contemplate. What would you find out about yourself that you didn't already know?

Youth is not about self-reflection; it's about changing the world and not about changing yourself. That is your younger version. Now as you age you carry with you the final version of another dynamic. It's different for everyone, but you know it when you discover a more profound sense of self and purpose. The chips land on the crap table of life in a different combination.

Finding purpose in your life is essential. For a while it might be your professional life, but everyone needs something that brings joy and personal fulfillment, something that brings together everything you know about yourself: your thoughts, ideas, values, dreams and emotions. This is your own personal goodie basket that aligns with who you are *now*, not with who you *once were*.

Finding meaning in life is the key to getting better with age. With meaning comes wisdom, self-knowledge and personal growth.

Sound good? Let's talk about ways to help you get there:

My favorite #1 way to find meaning in life is by finding passion. For some it might be traveling to exotic places, nurturing your grandchildren, writing your memoir or volunteering – whatever it is that gives you energy and fulfillment is your *great adventure* as you age. Aging is about taking control of your life.

Ask yourself what is it that you haven't done that you've always wanted to do. Journal the high points, bring to consciousness unresolved conflicts and gain a new perspective about living so you can move forward with grace and dignity. And most of all, forgive. Without forgiveness there can be no forward movement and no hope.

Become more present and aware so you can live a richer life. Paying attention to every action you take is important because it increases productivity, emotional intelligence and happiness. Spend some quiet time with yourself and release the unnecessary mental chatter going on in your head. It is then that you will be able to take pleasure in the smallest things in life.

Simplify your life is my personal favorite. Acquire less, desire less. Detaching from the material shifts your perspective to the importance of eliminating the unnecessary – that includes people, places and things that get in the way of clear intentions that keep you stuck in quicksand.

Always be authentic. Pay attention to your inner feelings rather than responding to the external world with all its mixed messages and false values. Know that your life is about the freedom to be yourself, to grow without the pressures to stay relevant and look gorgeous. You are relevant and gorgeous by the definition of who you are as a person – one of value and distinction.

As you get older, you do get better because the expression of yourself in all aspects of your life means that you have the freedom to make your own rules, discover your own rhythm and pace your life the way it suits you. Getting older means that you see yourself as the actual person you are, warts and all, always ready and willing and wiser.

IT'S TIME TO FORGIVE, ALREADY

If we're honest, we acknowledge that we have all harbored resentments, collected injustices, and have become angry over unimportant insults. I meditate. I burn candles. I drink green tea. And I still want to smack someone who offends me. It is challenging and completely exasperating to forgive.

It is challenging and completely exasperating to forgive someone – it might even be harder to forgive yourself. Forgiving is about letting go, surrendering, and moving forward. Forgiving not only clears the mind of negativity, but it is also crucial in resolving issues, communicating more effectively, providing empathy, and living a happier life yourself.

Without forgiveness there would be no history, no hope, and our species would have annihilated itself in endless retributions.

I'm proposing that you give yourself the gift of forgiveness when someone offends you. The study of yoga emphasizes the concept of *ahimsa*, a Sanskrit word that translates into non-violence – non-violence in thought, word or deed.

People can hurt you in many ways; however, you get to choose how to handle your emotions. You can get angry and hold on to negative emotions, or you can choose to meet the remark with forgiveness.

"Easier said than done to forgive," you may say. All right, I'll grant you that. Yet, the reality of the living experience is that your mind and your spirit makes decisions about how you want to live your life. *You are the only one responsible for shaping the life you want to live.*

It certainly is easer to give your mind a rest from the mental struggle of forgiving yourself and others. Sometimes this process can go on for decades. If you don't extract the best and most positive experiences of what life can offer you, you will spend your life mired in the negative.

Forgiveness focuses on the positive process of growth and development – the idea of experiencing your true self. The unforgiving state holds you back from living in the present. The power is in the now – not in the past.

Medical professionals agree that many of our long-term illnesses come as a result of emotional stress. Pent-up hostility and anger produce depression and anxiety along with a host of physical problems. The mental jail of negativity isn't a pleasant place to be.

I make it a practice to still my mind several times a day – a mini meditation, if you will, and release negative thoughts and ideas from my body and mind. I forgive myself for my mistakes, for speaking ill of someone, for judging someone, for labeling someone, for my negative feeling about my last relationship, for the fight with my son(s), for everything that happened and try to understand the lesson learned. Finally, I let go of my negative feelings and surrender to what is.

Research shows that you have, on average, three times more positive experiences than negative ones in a day, but your mind insists on focusing on the negatives. Letting go of negative thinking brought about by forgiveness enhances your well-being and leads to more joyful, more energetic and a much more satisfying life.

Finally, practicing forgiveness gives us all the ability to love, hope, and live with grace and dignity above all else in life.

LEAD ON

I gave myself a birthday present today even though my birthday isn't for another two weeks. I treated my boyfriend and myself to the movie *Suffragette*. I feared it might be a derivative retelling of the suffragette movement in the UK in the second decade of the 20th Century, but it was anything but derivative. Nothing about the fight to get the vote for women in the 20th Century is uninventive, unimaginable or uninspired.

For almost 100 years, women have been leading a crusade to obtain the vote. Through sacrifice, desperation, jail and even death, women have been driven by the need to be heard and be accounted for in society. We make up more than half of the world's population and in the underdeveloped part of the world most of us are silent.

Western civilization has acquiesced to the reality that women should be able to choose for themselves in all areas of life – at least in theory. However, there is still the debate in the United States about women having full control over our bodies and a view that the male gender is a far superior barometer of what we need and want. What an absurd notion! Males find women very complex, and the only way they can understand us is to manage us.

The movie was emotionally moving. I cried, and then cried again and again because it was such a compelling story. I wanted to be a suffragette and fight the battle to get the vote so that I could determine my own destiny.

But I do control my destiny and I am one of the lucky women in the world who can say that. I don't suffer degradation and food deprivation, nor do I live in squalor or poverty. I am able to get an education, to vote, to choose my profession, to marry who I wish, to raise my children the way I see fit, to determine my lifestyle choices and even to die with dignity.

Suffragette was so powerful a view of women struggling to achieve their natural rights that it captured once again the vivid male stereotypes and projections and paternalistic thinking that have produced a female underclass. The message of the movie was a grateful reminder that my life and the lives of an educated western world have come a long way toward civilized discourse and are getting closer to unequivocal parity

Although I have lived a little more than 7 decades gaining some knowledge and insight about the human condition, I acknowledge that I am still in an ongoing process of learning about the state of human existence.

Today I made yet another intention to stay aware and focused about what constitutes parity in society for women. Although I can't force the energy toward equality to move at a faster pace and instantly make the world a level playing field where rights for both men and women are equal, I can *lead on* by example and lend an awareness to the plight of women who have no way to manifest their destiny. Knowledge is power and the knowledge of the history of how women struggled and fought to have an equal voice in society is germane to the way we conduct ourselves and lend our support to those who have no platform for their agenda.

So happy birthday to me in my 72nd year. I've given myself yet another wake-up call, another gift by renewing my intention to be all that I can be and use my knowledge and skills to influence other women to maximize their human potential so that they may *lead on* in their lives.

5 WAYS TO LEAVE A GREAT LEGACY

The discussion of *leaving a legacy* has come up in conversation recently among my friends and family. Most of my friends are almost or just past mid-century age, and my sons and daughters-in-law are almost 40 years old or older. There must something in the water.

I thought about the concept of legacy when my grandchildren were born ten years ago when I was 61. It seems my friends and family are way ahead of me on the idea of a life well lived and what they will leave future generations. One of my sons said to me the other day, "My work is done on this earth. I have three wonderful children." I tried not to tear up.

The idea of leaving a legacy is the need or the desire to be remembered for what you have contributed to the world. In some cases, that contribution can be so special that the universe is unalterably changed.

However, most mere mortals walking the earth will leave a modest legacy that won't necessarily change the world. But any legacy either large or small does leave a lasting footprint that will be remembered by those whose lives you touched.

You hope your life matters in some way. Mine does. I've been teaching since the age of 22 and teaching is my legacy, my contribution that hopefully enlightened the lives of my students whether they became actors, scientists, doctors, mothers or yogis. Teaching is a gift that keeps on giving because it leads me to other learning and knowing experiences that I share with others.

My purposeful legacy is my family: 2 sons and 5 grandchildren. I hope I am fully present to be the best that I can be as a mother and grandmother. I also hope that I am leaving a legacy as a good daughter, a loyal and loving sister, and friend.

"Carve your name on hearts, not tombstones. A legacy is etched into the minds of others and the stories they share about you." ~ Shannon L. Alder

Of course, leaving a legacy is a personal matter. But here is some food for thought:

Support the People and Causes that are Important to You
My best friend of decades once asked me what I thought was the most important attribute of friendship. I told her that there isn't any more wonderful feeling in life than making the choice to sustain loyalty to a friend by lovingly supporting everything that is good and right about that person's life.

My friend was an advocate of a few major causes in the city we resided in and I supported those causes, too, as she supported mine. Although we parted ways when I moved out of the city, she would always reach out to me and remember my work, my life and my family.

Reflect and Decide What is Most Important in your Life
When you review your life's journey, several ideas may come to mind: did you grow and perhaps transform your life, make changes when you needed to, find your truth, inspire others, become a leader or influence others? Touching lives and exemplifying a truthful path is paramount to living a joyful and purposeful life. Your legacy will live on.

Share Your Blessings
I was walking two dogs the other day – one dog was totally blind and the other dog stubbornly knew her mind. I stopped suddenly in the middle of my son's beautiful neighborhood to observe with wonder the late afternoon thunderclouds bulging out from the mountains. I thought of all the blessings I have in life and how I try to be mindful of sharing with others the richness of my life. I have been given abundance and such is my fate.

And it is my legacy to give back this abundance to others. Everyone has blessings to share, even if it's a simple smile of acknowledgement.

Be a Mentor to Others
A mentor by definition is a more experienced or more knowledgeable person with an area of expertise. Everyone has some significant truth to impart to others that will guide the less experienced. The mentoring/mentee relationship involves personal development and support.

This process involves an exchange of knowledge complimented by communication and psychological and/or social support that is relevant to sustaining a healthy mindset. Sometimes these relationships last a lifetime, even when the mentee has moved on to influence others.

Pursue Your Passions Because They Are Infectious
Your passions are your legacy. Passion comes from an outpouring of the interests and ideas that make a difference in your life. Finding and pursuing your passion allows you to see your destiny clearly. That's what happened to me with yoga and dancing tango.

I can attest to the fact that life won't be any fun if you don't pursue your passions to the fullest. It's contagious. It's religious. Don't miss the opportunity to pursue your passions and continue to look for new adventures.

Leaving a legacy is an important part of your life's work. A legacy develops from a life dedicated to self-reflection and purpose. What will be revealed and what will endure is a truthful and value-driven body of living.

NEVER THE END

I'm still a rock star and sexy, smart and strong no matter my age. I choose to keep dancing Argentine tango and continue to write and blog like a junkie. I choose to keep loving with an open heart, recognize my vulnerabilities with joy, and I choose to continue to enrich my life. That's my mission, that's my mantra and I'm sticking to it because *I'm the boss of me.*

Made in the USA
San Bernardino, CA
01 April 2016